Labour Inspectors in Italy

Rebecca Paraciani

Labour Inspectors in Italy

Between Discretion and Institutional Pressure

palgrave
macmillan

Rebecca Paraciani
Department of Sociology and Business Law
University of Bologna, Strada Maggiore 45
Bologna, Italy

ISBN 978-3-031-37996-3 ISBN 978-3-031-37997-0 (eBook)
https://doi.org/10.1007/978-3-031-37997-0

This Palgrave Macmillan imprint is published by the registered company Springer Nature Switzerland AG.
The registered company address is: Gewerbestrasse 11, 6330 Cham, Switzerland

To Dino, my incredible son

Acknowledgements

Firstly, I would like to thank the labour inspectors who participated with enthusiasm and curiosity, making this research possible.

I would also like to thank Sharla Plant, the editor of this work, who believed that this book was possible.

This work is also the result of the input from Professor Roberto Rizza, the supervisor for my PhD, and Dr Kim Loyes, who was the supervisor for my visiting research period. Without their precise and careful help, I would not have succeeded in completing this book.

Thank you to Tatiana Saruis, Dario Raspanti, and Daniela Leonardi: my street (level) mates.

Thank you to Ilaria Pitti, Alessandro Bozzetti, Stella Volturo, and Valeria Piro: we're having fun, but we're still not happy.

Thanks to my dad and mom for always being there and to my sister Camilla for being my friend. Thanks to Tiziana and Renato, for sharing their time. Thank you Giacomo: for everything and forever.

Keywords

Labour inspectors • Street-level bureaucracy • Neo-institutionalism • Labour exploitation • Ethnography • Vignette study • Italian case

Contents

List of Figures

List of Tables

CHAPTER 1

Introduction

Abstract This chapter introduces the main purpose of the book. It details the stages that led to the development of the research questions and the importance of seeking answers through the lens of street-level bureaucracy. The research questions that guided the analysis are as follows: (a) What institutional pressures exist in the organisational field of labour inspections, and what are their consequences?; (b) How does labour inspectors' discretion manifest in their interventions, and what impact does it have in determining the severity of the cases to be handled?; (c) Why are similar work irregularities treated differently? The book aims to answer these research questions by making an original contribution to street-level research, introducing the analysis of the organisational field of workplace controls, and merging the street-level perspective with neo-institutionalist theory.

Keywords Labour inspectors • Italy • Street-level bureaucracy • Neo-institutionalism • Work irregularities

R. Paraciani, *Labour Inspectors in Italy*,
https://doi.org/10.1007/978-3-031-37997-0_1

Lunch break.

Inspector Pino[1] tells me that discretion does not exist in their work: "If some colleague tells you otherwise and says we are free to choose the solution we want, there is little you can do: He is acting illegally. He must surely be breaking some rule, some law, some directive. We are not free!" Inspector Arianna suggests that I do not listen to him; that Pino is too cynical. She replies, "We are people first and then labour inspectors. We are not robots. We must think, take decisions, make assessments, and, afterwards, act in the right way for that situation."

Pino laughs. (Field note, May 2017)

This book aims to investigate the operational practices of labour inspectors engaged in handling work irregularities that lie on the border of *severe* and *non-severe labour exploitation*. The analytical perspective adopted is that of *street-level bureaucracy*, as introduced in a series of studies by Lipsky (1980) that continues to exert a strong influence on analyses focusing on the implementation processes of public interest policies. This approach assigns a key role to professional figures who interact directly with citizens and have the power to dispense benefits or sanctions to them.

To consider labour inspectors street-level bureaucrats means analysing the ways in which these public actors translate institutionally developed laws, norms, and guidelines into their daily practices. In this process, they exercise discretion in their operational practices by making choices that balance the formal norms with the resources available to them. In this book, we explore the ways in which labour inspectors deal with labour exploitation and its severity.

Studying labour inspectors' discretion was not the starting point of the research journey but a circumstance that came by chance. There were three moments that constituted this change of course: First, it was very difficult to find an unambiguous definition of "labour exploitation." Second, the legal definition could not be applied to *Article 603bis of the Italian Criminal Code*, which is the article that regulates illegal labour brokering and labour exploitation within the Italian legal system. In most situations, these are cases that border on servitude and slavery that are closely related to human trafficking. Finally, the third moment was a labour inspector's intervention during a seminar on labour exploitation in the tourism sector, which was titled "What I see when I go." Among the

[1] Inspector Pino's name, as well as all the names of the inspectors that are mentioned in this book, are pseudonyms in order to protect the privacy of the research participants.

issues considered, he highlighted the difficulties of enforcing formal regulations but also the various possible alternatives to inspection and, above all, the various dilemmas that he had to handle daily.

In the same vein, Lipsky (1980) detailed some of the *professional dilemmas* that labour inspectors could encounter: If a colleague transgresses some rules, is it better to talk to the colleague directly or to notify a supervisor? Can a labour inspector decide to not initiate an inspection? If a worker arrives at closing time, should the inspector ask the person who intends to file a complaint to return the next day or record the request for action? If an inspector witnesses a violation that is considered minor, will they turn a blind eye or dispense a penalty? These and other scenarios are examples of the situations in which one decision has consequences for others and in which important values conflict (Kaptein et al., 2005; Maesschalck, 2005). Therefore, to resolve these issues, the decision space of street-level bureaucrats as actors within the *policy-making* process is relevant.

Street-level bureaucrats do not just do what they want or what is asked of them as they would often find themselves managing situations that are unlikely to occur again by using the resources at their disposal (Vinzant & Crothers, 1998; Brodkin, 2012). Studying labour inspectors' decision-making processes means shedding light on the *black box* of policies' implementation and trying to understand the ways in which labour exploitation takes shape. Labour inspectors are an understudied group of street-level bureaucrats, but their role is relevant in the determination of labour policies: As stated by Van de Walle and Raaphorst (2019), labour inspectors have a crucial role in enforcing rules and standards, and their role has changed. For this reason, it is important to explore the social dynamics of the interactions between inspectors and their inspectees.

This book aims to make an original contribution to the street-level perspective by introducing the analysis levels for the organisational field of workplace controls. The starting point is Rice's (2013) study on caseworkers' roles in shaping the outcomes of policies and the objectives of the welfare state as well as the extent to which these objectives are increasing in the *activation era*. Rice (2013) proposes the connection between the street-level approach and the institutionalist theory, thus laying the foundation for a micro-institutionalist theory of welfare policy implementation. Moreover, Rice (2019) proposes using a Mertonian perspective to explain why certain street-level bureaucratic jobs are more important within organisations or policy delivery systems. This is to overcome many of the criticisms that have been levelled at the street-level approach, in that it is only a lens for micro analyses of interactions. Instead, Rice (2019) broadens the lens by considering not only individual and organisational dynamics (Brodkin, 2012) but also institutional ones, which have repercussions not only on the form that norms take but also on their implementation. In the wake of this multilevel perspective, a neo-institutionalist lens was adopted according to Powell's and DiMaggio's (1983) analytical reasoning, which entailed adopting the concept of the organisational field to refer to the heterogeneous constellation of actors who influence and are influenced by the dynamics of the field itself. Thus, several actors present in the organisational field of workplace controls were identified and their interactions investigated. I used this analytical lens during my PhD research and when writing an article (Paraciani & Rizza, 2021) with my supervisor, Professor Rizza, on labour inspectors' discretionary power and the tools available in the institutional field of domestic work. The results were interesting in that they accounted for individuals' different adaptations to identical organisational or policy contexts.

The research questions that guided this analysis are as follows: (a) What institutional pressures exist in the organisational field of labour inspections, and what are their consequences? (b) How does labour inspectors' discretion manifest in their interventions, and what impact does it have in determining the severity of the cases to be handled? and (c) Why are similar work irregularities treated differently?

To answer these research questions, a qualitative methodology was used by integrating different techniques with the aim of profoundly interacting with the object of study. The "behind the scenes" of this book comprises a three-year PhD study. First, a documentary analysis was conducted to reconstruct the work completed by labour inspectors as well as their spaces of discretion, formal priorities, reporting tools, levels of autonomy, and possible interpretations. However, these were not the only aspects investigated as the analysis also extended to the context, thereby allowing for a regulatory and historical analysis, which translated into determining the structure of the organisational field of workplace controls as well as an understanding of the actors and their relationships. Second, nine months of ethnographic study was conducted within a local office of the Italian National Labour Inspectorate in the form of observing street-level bureaucrats in three different decisional moments called *rooms of discretion*. Finally, the preliminary observations resulting from the ethnographic study were expanded on through interviews with the labour inspectors using vignettes: Three plausible intervention request scenarios were created in order to compare similar irregularities within different productive sectors.

In Chap. 2, starting with the theoretical framework of street-level bureaucracy, the meaning of "discretion" is questioned by focusing on dilemmas faced by an understudied category of street-level bureaucrats: labour inspectors. An integration between this analytical level and the organisational dimension is subsequently proposed, thereby presenting the analytical tool of this research: the organisational field of workplace controls.

Chapter 3 then details Italian case studies by first presenting the legislation on labour exploitation to highlight the fine line between severe and non-severe forms of exploitation, which are the categories into which the work irregularities observed during this study are divided. In this continuum, the labour inspectors' discretionary power is particularly relevant. This chapter then highlights the transformations that have occurred in the Italian National Labour Inspectorate and emphasises the actors that influence and are influenced by the field's dynamics. In the last section, the institutional pressures of the organisational field of workplace controls are presented.

Chapter 4 is purely ethnographic and sheds light on the ways in which discretion is manifested within the observed Italian National Labour Inspectorate headquarters. Using field notes and other material collected during the nine months of participant observation, rooms of discretion are described, which are the physical places in which labour inspectors make their decisions. It delineates the ways in which discretion is manifested and exercised in the physical places in which *bureaucratic encounters* take place (Jilke & Tummers, 2018; Leonardi et al., 2021). If an interaction occurs between a street-level bureaucrat and a user, thereby making politics concrete and allowing it to make sense, the spaces in which the meetings take place also become important: The description of the observed site's ergonomics is useful for describing the relationships and interactions that occur in those rooms. This chapter then ends with the preliminary findings that are analysed using the vignette method, as detailed in the following chapter.

Chapter 5 presents the main results obtained through the adopted interpretative framework. In particular, the three main types of isomorphic pressures affecting the organisational field of workplace controls are described as well as how these pressures affect the ways in which inspectors act in their spaces of discretion. The data from the interviews were analysed using the vignette method, which allowed the street-level approach to be restored to its "comparative essence" (Lipsky, 2010, XIX) by comparing similar work irregularities within different productive sectors: logistics; domestic work; and restaurant. The use of this tool allowed for the creation of plausible scenarios through which labour inspectors' daily experiences could be expanded upon.

Chapter 6 is devoted to discussing the relationship between labour inspectors and formal regulatory instruments by detailing how the rooms of discretion and the ways in which they are used give shape and meaning to certain social phenomena by encouraging new research perspectives.

References

Brodkin, E. Z. (2012). Reflections on street-level bureaucracy: Past, present, and future. *Public Administration Review, 72*(6), 940–949.

DiMaggio, P., & Powell, W. (1983). The Iron Cage Revisited: Institutional isomorphism and collective rationality in organizational fields. *American Sociological Review, 48*, 147–160.

Jilke, S., & Tummers, L. (2018). Which clients are deserving of help? A theoretical model and experimental test. *Journal of Public Administration Research and Theory, 28*(2), 226–238.

Kaptein, M., Huberts, L., Avelino, S., & Lasthuizen, K. (2005). Demonstrating ethical leadership by measuring ethics: A survey of US public servants. *Public Integrity, 7*(4), 299–311.

Leonardi, D., Paraciani, R., & Raspanti, D. (2021). A strategy is necessary. The policy–client conflict within different relational asymmetries: a comparison at the street-level. *International Journal of Sociology and Social Policy, 41*(13/14), 81–95.

Lipsky, M. (1980). *Street level bureaucracy: Dilemmas of the individual in public services.* Russell Sage Foundation.

Lipsky M. (2010). *Street level bureaucracy. Dilemmas of the individual in public services* 30th Anniversary Expanded Edition. Russell Sage Foundation.

Maesschalck, J. (2005). The use of the ethical climate questionnaire in the public sector: An empirical assessment. In *Ethics and integrity of governance: The first transatlantic dialogue.* Leuven.

Paraciani, R., & Rizza, R. (2021). When the workplace is the home: Labour inspectors' discretionary power in the field of domestic work–an institutional analysis. *Journal of Public Policy, 41*(1), 1–16.

Rice, D. (2013). Street-Level Bureaucrats and the Welfare State: toward a micro-institutionalist theory of policy implementation. *Administration & Society, 45*(9), 1038–1062.
Rice, D. (2019). Adopting an institutional view in street-level bureaucracy research. In P. Hupe (Ed.), *Research handbook on street-level bureaucracy* (pp. 70–85). Edward Elgar Publishing.
Van de Walle, S., & Raaphorst, N. (Eds.). (2019). *Inspectors and enforcement at the front line of government*. Palgrave Macmillan.
Vinzant, J., & Crothers, L. (1998). *Street-level leader- ship: Discretion and legitimacy in front-line public service*. Georgetown University Press.

CHAPTER 2

Discretion Within Institutional Contexts: Italian Labour Inspectors in the Organisational Field of Workplace Controls

Abstract This chapter presents the underlying theory of this book. Using the theoretical framework of street-level bureaucracy, the organisational field of workplace controls is presented. The various definitions of "discretion" and "street-level bureaucrats" are provided, after which the inclusion of street-level bureaucrats at the centre of this research is discussed. Labour inspectors are an understudied professional category as research on this professional figure is scarce and is mostly concentrated in the United States and Northern Europe. Therefore, labour inspectors in Italy were studied using a neo-institutionalist perspective by analysing their practices and the organisational context through the lens of the organisational field of workplace controls, which is a neo-institutionalist analytical tool. Indeed, the last section outlines the Italian organisational field of workplace controls.

Keywords Street-level bureaucracy • Discretion • Labour inspectors • Organisational field of workplace controls • Italian Labour Inspectorate

R. Paraciani, *Labour Inspectors in Italy*,
https://doi.org/10.1007/978-3-031-37997-0_2

2.1 Street-Level Bureaucracy and Discretion

The term "street-level bureaucracy" was coined by Lipsky (1980) to highlight the importance of the discretion employed by professionals in public agencies when translating laws, regulations, standards, and guidelines into practice. Acting at the "street level," they often adapt very general rules to specific cases, interpreting them according to the circumstances in which they are operating and adopting some autonomy in the use of these tools. Through interaction with a citizen's specific problem, they have the power to determine "the quantity and quality of benefits and sanctions provided by the public agency to which they belong" (Lipsky, 1980, p. 13).

Street-level bureaucrats are social workers, teachers, police officers, labour inspectors, revenue agency inspectors, and generally the professionals who employ their own operational strategies in the process of implementing public interest policies while working within public agencies and partly allocating goods and services (Brodkin, 2011). Thus, their actions embody a paradox in that they must treat all citizens as if they were on the same level, but they are simultaneously forced to take charge of an individual's problem, choosing how to allocate resources to resolve the situation in the appropriate way. There are two constitutive characteristics that public agency personnel must have:

1. They must directly interact with citizens for the purpose of dispensing sanctions or benefits on behalf of the institution to which they belong, representing the institution in the interaction between the institution and the citizen; and
2. In carrying out this task, the public agency personnel have a certain degree of discretionary power at their disposal, which is ineradicable as it is the essence of their work (Lipsky, 1980).

Therefore, studying street-level bureaucracy means analysing how public institutions translate laws, rules, and regulations into operational practice as well as the ways in which the tools of intervention are adapted to the specific problems they face and the conditions under which they must act (Saruis, 2015).

The interaction with the citizen and their problem makes the position of these bureaucrats "unique and influential" (Meyers & Vorsanger, 2003, p. 153). They are "agents of social control" (Lipsky, 1980, p. 4) who, although not operating at the top of the organisational hierarchical ladder, play a key role in shaping public policy (Meyers & Vorsanger, 2003; Hupe & Hill, 2007). They are co-producers of policy, not mere implementers, and thus contribute to creating and maintaining the normative order of society (Maynard-Moody & Musheno, 2003). Indeed, the decisions they make are translated into public policies.

A founding element of these professionals' work is discretion, which is an inevitable and central condition of the street-level approach. Those who work at the street-level, therefore, play a very delicate role as they need to manage the needs of the organisation for which they work (in its various articulations) as well as those of the users to whom they provide customised responses based on the available resources (Ham & Hill, 1986; Saruis, 2015). Thus, practitioners' role is full of contradictions. They experience different types of pressures and find themselves having to mediate between these tensions, not only reproducing institutional structures but also introducing elements of change (Giddens, 1984).

Discretion is not synonymous with arbitrariness nor freedom nor, in a negative connotation, anarchy; it is a multifaceted concept (Hupe, 2019). Hupe (2013) analyses discretion from legal, sociological, and political perspectives. From the legal point of view, discretionary power seems inevitable: "The existence of rules implies discretion, and, at the same time, the existence of discretionary space makes rules necessary" (Hawkins, 1992, p. 12). These rules need to be interpreted to give the formal rule meaning and to enable those who use them to make choices based on those rules. In the legal definition, discretion is a gap that opens between rules as choices are made (Dworkin, 1978). Sociologists have addressed discretion within organisational and administrative contexts (Merton, 1940) by considering the contrast between professional autonomy and the limits imposed by bureaucracy (Freidson, 1970). Hill (1969) studies discretion in the implementation of public policies through social interaction, and Lipsky (1980) introduced the concept of street-level bureaucracy, referring to the alienation of these professionals and the coping techniques used to handle this alienation, thereby shedding light on the ambivalence of discretionary power. According to political scientists, public discourse almost never coincides with public action (Dixon et al., 2012). The political-administrative cycle is not exhausted at the level of policy-making, but the users of these policy instruments act as filters in the application of certain public interventions (Brodkin, 1997; Paraciani & Saruis, 2019).

Although discretion is "an idea that is difficult to define" (Evans, 2016, p. 2), scholars have defined this concept in a few ways. Among the most widely cited definitions of public actors' discretionary power during the policy implementation phase is Davis's (Davis, 1969) statement that a public official exercises discretion whenever the actual limits of their power give them the freedom to choose one of many possible actions. Smith (1981) distinguishes between *de jure* and *de facto discretion*, with the former including Davis's definition and referring to the authority to act and decide that is conferred on the practitioner by a formal rule and the latter referring to the power that is not officially recognised and may also be related to the absence of effective control. Brodkin (2011) defines "discretion" as a response determined not only by the street-level bureaucrat and their interactions with users but also by specific organisational conditions. Dubois (2010) also goes beyond the micro view of the street-level bureaucrat by considering the relationship between the bureaucrat and the institutional context. The author asserts that the way these professionals use discretion is influenced by (a) the roles they encounter and disagree with in the course of interacting with users; (b) the need to manage tensions and ensure consensus while maintaining institutional order; and (c) the ways in which institutions are transformed.

Street-level bureaucrats, interacting directly with citizens' needs, cannot simply implement the measures stipulated by regulations but must interpret the rule according to the different interests that come into play, thereby risking a production or reproduction of inequalities that can result in some accessing certain services while others do not (Dubois, 2010). Maynard-Moody and Musheno (2003) liken formal norms to a sea that those who work at street level must navigate, and to do so they inevitably find themselves also applying their own moral, not just legal, values. Winter (2003) refers to objective discretion by considering the different ways in which rules can be applied and the subjective discretion that is needed when there are different coping strategies employed to manage the workload. Ricucci (2005) introduces a yardstick for measuring discretion: low discretion occurs from the organisation controlling more of the decisions; and high discretion entails the practitioners being able to make decisions according to their professional judgement. Therefore, this is a broad notion that is difficult to circumscribe.

Grouping together various definitions, discretion has three meanings that are not mutually exclusive but that complement one another (Evans & Harris, 2004; Kazepov & Barberis, 2012; Paraciani & Saruis, 2019):

1. Discretion *within* the law and the procedures: The street-level bureaucrat uses discretionary power that is confined by the limits set by the formal normative frame of reference assigned to them by the norm itself.
2. Discretion *among* the law and the procedures: The street-level bureaucrat interprets and constructs the norms, inserting themselves within the spaces of ambiguity and the overlap between norms to the fill gaps and uncertainties in the formal regulatory system.
3. Discretion *out of* the law and the procedures: The street-level bureaucrat violates the stipulations set forth in the formal regulations to preclude or allow users access to the service.

Thus, discretion is a tool through which the complexity of reality can be managed with practical solutions, and analysing it allows for understanding what happens inside the black box of implementation. The street-level perspective has allowed for a change in the understanding of discretionary power as a mere regulatory violation and the perception of public service work as merely executive by highlighting the relevance of discretionary power, which is indispensable for managing complex situations in policy-making (Brodkin, 2008).

The literature identifies several reasons why discretion is an indispensable tool for these practitioners:

1. The resources available are often insufficient to meet all requests for intervention (Lipsky, 2010). Discretion is directly proportional to the limited resources available to street-level bureaucrats, who evaluate requests for intervention and decide how to strike a balance between the available resources and the problems to be solved (Ellis, 2011).
2. The goals of the organisations in which street-level bureaucrats work and the regulatory tools they use are often vague and unclear. The lack of a shared definition results in practitioners needing to exercise increased amounts of discretion (Brodkin, 2008).
3. There is an informative asymmetry between street-level bureaucrats and citizens, which contributes to practitioners having to exercise more discretion, especially when service users are considered fragile. This asymmetry can relate to power, cultural resources, and language skills (Raspanti & Saruis, 2022).

Therefore, the decision-making autonomy of those who find themselves implementing policies appears to be natural and indispensable when resolving professional dilemmas (Lipsky, 2010). An example of a professional dilemma is an official who does not perform a same-sex civil union for religious reasons, a doctor being a conscientious objector, a traffic official who, instead of ticketing for an infraction, only issues a warning, or a social worker who decides whether to provide benefits based on the limited resources available. One of the main consequences of discretionary power is creating groups of people who are either included or excluded in terms of who can access the available services and under what conditions. This is why Brodkin (2011) calls street-level bureaucrats de facto policy-makers.

The implementation of different strategies depends on three factors: individual decision-makers' characteristics; the organisational and extra-organisational context; and the type of customer (Prottas, 1979; Scott, 1997; Vinzant & Crothers, 1998). Several studies have analysed the effect of individual decision-makers' characteristics, with Miller (1967) being among the first to study the relationship between job alienation and incentives for bureaucrats with varying degrees of professionalisation. He concludes that those who held a higher level of professionalisation were more likely to deviate from formal standards and rules. Several studies conclude that norms as well as front-line workers' moral values and levels of professionalisation are indispensable elements that should be considered when analysing decision-making processes. Gender variables, educational background, ethnicity, and religious beliefs are also important in this regard (Walker, 1993; Meyers & Vorsanger, 2003; Maynard-Moody & Musheno, 2003; Watkins-Hayes, 2013). The organisation's structure, the workload, and the rules and performance evaluation criteria also have an influence on street-level bureaucrats' decision-making processes (Kelly, 1994; Scott, 1997; Brodkin, 2008), with Brodkin stating that "street-level bureaucrats do not just do what they want or what the organization wants, but they often find themselves forced to do what they can" (Brodkin, 2008, p. 24). In this way, their choices end up characterising the concrete interventions delivered, thereby becoming the very essence of the policies created.

2.2 Labour Inspectors as Street-Level Bureaucrats

Labour inspectors, as street-level bureaucrats, must decide on the solutions for work irregularities. Working in control and supervisory agencies, labour inspectors "decide who to sanction, determining the nature and quality of the sanction" (Lipsky, 2010, p. 13). Despite their being effectively street-level bureaucrats, they remain an understudied category of professionals (Van de Walle & Raaphorst, 2019). Moreover, they are often studied together with other categories of inspectors, such as tax inspectors and restaurant inspectors (Raaphorst & Loyens, 2020) but not as professionals whose daily work can influence the quality of a country's labour market (Van Berkel & Knies, 2018; Loyens & Paraciani, 2023). Piore and Schrank (2008, 2018) determine the role these actors play in ensuring decent work conditions within complex environments in Latin America and the United States by studying the relationship between business practices and standards of "decent work," ultimately concluding that Latin American labour professionals' discretion was characterised by a vagueness that was echoed in the understanding of decent work, which was considered a "meaningless" (Schrank & Piore, 2007, p. 20) concept by the authors. Their working methods and goals were defined by the practices embedded in the inspectorate's culture and passed from one generation of inspectors to another without formalisation. Other studies (e.g., Nielsen, 2006; Loyens, 2016) investigate how personal and contextual aspects influence labour inspectors' decision-making. These studies, conducted using ethnographic methods, show that the perception of the severity of certain situations determines the priorities in the resolutions provided. They also highlight how the resolution of a case is not for the benefit of the victim but is the outcome of other aspects; for example, the number of arrests and cases resolved is an indicator of the quality of the inspector's performance.

Several scholars agree that inspectors have considerable discretion at their disposal (e.g., Gilboy, 1992) as they decide when to conduct inspections, how thoroughly to conduct investigations, and how to interact with witnesses and employers (Goosensen & van der Voort, 2009; Goosensen,

2021). They also have discretion in terms of deciding the severity of the penalty and, more generally, the results of inspections (Wiering, 1999; May & Wood, 2003; Nielsen, 2006). There are several studies on the ways in which labour inspectors manage their discretion. Fineman (1998) uses an ethnographic study to highlight the tensions in the situations in which these professionals find themselves, including operational practices as well as the demands resulting from formal regulations and the organisation. Moreover, the ways in which these actors move within a context dominated by business logic and how their decisions are conditioned by market rules are explicated (Fineman, 1998, p. 71).

Most studies on labour inspectors' policy implementation focus on the identification of operational styles. Reiss (1984) highlights an approach characterised by two operational styles: a compliance-oriented operational style, the purpose of which is to remediate irregularities, and a sanctioning style, which involves making use of sanctions as deterrents. This is a simplification that Wiering (1999) develops by introducing two variables that guide action: the degree of goal orientation and the degree of rule orientation. Kagan (1997) considers the two levels of administrative responsiveness (i.e., active or inactive) and the two styles of punishment (i.e., delaying or cooperative) and relates them to four influencing factors: legislation, task specificity, political environment, and leadership style. However, these strands of research have faced criticism (Loyens, 2015) in that they are considered too reductive of the complexity of reality and they are often at odds with each other. A second strand of research analyses how labour inspectors face similar professional challenges in different ways and concludes that the reality is not always consistent with the official goals decided at the ministerial or organisational level but depends on how officials interpret norms and situations (Chan, 1998; Raaphorst, 2018). Labour inspectors, through their daily practices, translate policies to counteract work irregularities using concrete actions by choosing how to handle requests that need action, what prominence to give to individual cases, whether to conduct the investigation, and how to do it.

2.3 The Neo-institutionalist Approach: The Organisational Field of Workplace Controls

If street-level bureaucracy dissects practitioners' various discretionary choices made in the course of implementing policies based on formal rules, highlighting how they are translated into concrete practices on the basis of available resources, the neo-institutionalist perspective (DiMaggio & Powell, 1991) allows us to go beyond the micro level by integrating multiple levels of analysis and considering the organisations in the field within which they operate. The organisational field consists of "a collection of organizations that, taken together, constitute a recognized area of institutional life: suppliers, consumers of resources and products, controlling agencies, and other organizations that produce similar products or services" (Powell and DiMaggio 48). Organisational fields are formed when actors of different types, through frequent exchanges and interactions, become interdependent on each other. The existence of an organisational field results in similar logics of action as well as the acquisition of a similar vocabulary and similar systems of meaning, leading to parts of the field considering some actions legitimate and others illegitimate. This tendency to converge does not mean that there is cultural homogeneity such that this relational space is free of differences and conflicts. It does mean, however, that an environment is created within which actors are able to recognise each other through their differences and conflicts. Reasoning in terms of the field means reasoning in relational terms (Bourdieu, 1999), leading to cognitive, symbolic, and normative forces coming into play with which organisations and actors in various capacities need to comply. Most research using the organisational field analytical tool shows how organisations first tend to seek legitimacy to ensure their survival. The neo-institutional lens highlights how organisations are complex and socially constructed systems. Indeed, when practices, roles, and organisational forms become legitimate and appropriate ways of acting are determined for members of an organisation, the organisation's institutionalisation takes place, and certain organisational forms become embedded in actors' values and beliefs. Scott (1997) states that studying organisations is not necessarily about determining which organisational model is effective but, more importantly, is about understanding why an organisation decides to implement a given model as well as the ways in which it is changed and reproduced. In this process, the institutional environment in which the organisation is rooted has fundamental importance (Meyer & Rowan, 1977). Organisations, as part of the social context, are influenced by socially sedimented and shared beliefs that condition the organisational model. Thus, organisations are susceptible to pressures from the external environment to which they adapt through processes of institutional isomorphism, which is a conceptual tool introduced by DiMaggio and Powell (1983) to describe a converging force that leads to organisations assuming similar forms in order to gain legitimacy and political power. The processes of isomorphism are not indistinct, with Powell and DiMaggio identifying three processes: *coercive*, which entails an organisation being subject to external pressures, such as legal constraints, but also cultural constraints present within the social system, which force it to conform; *mimetic*, in which uncertain situations are handled by imitating already identified solutions as everyone acts a certain way for a reason; and *normative* isomorphism, which arises from professionalisation processes aimed at improving certain practices as change is generated not by uncertainty but by an intention to improve and being aware that new practices are superior to old ones (Bonazzi, 2002, 2004). Adopting a field perspective means giving meaning and significance to processes as well as specifying the relationships between actors, organisations, and the institutional environment.

For the purposes of this research, it is appropriate to reiterate an important aspect of neo-institutionalist analysis: The focus is on organisational actors' cognitive processes, their practices, and the pressures that the institutional environment exerts on organisations and organisational action. However, although neo-institutionalist scholars have stated that the role of the micro level needs to be more explicit in unravelling how the institutionalisation of certain practices occurs within an organisation (DiMaggio & Powell, 1991; Zucker, 1987), efforts in this direction have seen limited progress and have only become popular in recent years (Colyvas, 2007; Rice, 2013, 2019). Integrating street-level bureaucracy with the neo-institutionalist perspective can help derive an understanding of the dynamics at work within the organisational field of workplace controls (Paraciani & Rizza, 2021). The actors in the organisational field of workplace controls are diverse, and their interactions are continuous. They are control agencies and *inspection bodies*, companies and employers, workers with irregular work statuses, labour associations, consumers, *the Ministry of Labour and Social Policy*, journalists, and information agencies that help directly shape the field. The first actor is the Ministry of Labour and Social Policy. Among its other responsibilities, it is tasked with establishing labour priorities, monitoring safety and hygiene conditions in workplaces, and ensuring an annual number of inspections for each production sector. Other institutional actors active in the field are the inspection bodies. The Italian National Labour Inspectorate was reorganised into a single agency in January 2017 by Legislative Decree 149/2015, which ensures uniformity in all supervisory personnels' work procedures, including not only the Ministry's inspectors, but also the inspectors from the National Institute for Insurance against Accidents at Work (INAIL) and the National Institute for Social Security (INPS), both of which are tasked with protecting workers' health, combatting undeclared and irregular work, and verifying the regular contribution that needs to be paid by employers. The National Labour Inspectorate has organisational and accounting autonomy but is constantly monitored by the Ministry of Labour and Social Policy, which, in addition to providing guidance on objectives, monitors the inspectorates' work and use of financial resources. For these purposes, a *General Directorate* was established in the Ministry of Labour and Social Policy by Legislative Decree 124/2004 and was tasked with directing, planning, and coordinating inspection activities in the areas of labour relations, social legislation (including social security institutions), and essential labour services. The Directorate General translates the directions issued by the Ministry of Labour and Social Policy into operational directives and then ensures uniformity in supervisory bodies' actions, thereby guaranteeing the unified exercise and monitoring of supervisory activities. The Directorate General for Management and Information and Communications Technology is also responsible for planning and managing inspectors' training and refresher courses.

The National Labour Inspectorate has a hierarchical articulation within the territory. There are four Interregional Labour Directorates (DIL) in

Milan, Venice, Rome, and Naples, which are considered the headquarters: The Milanese DIL coordinates the activities of the inspectorates in Liguria, Lombardy, Piedmont, and Valle D'Aosta; the DIL in Venice coordinates the functions of the inspectorates in Emilia-Romagna, Friuli-Venezia Giulia, Marche, and Veneto; the interregional headquarters in Rome control the territorial offices of the inspectorate in Abruzzo, Lazio, Sardinia, Tuscany, and Umbria; and the DIL in Naples is responsible for monitoring inspectorate activities in Basilicata, Campania, Calabria, Molise, and Puglia. DILs also play the role of Territorial Labour Inspectorates (ITLs), previously Territorial Labour Directorates, in the areas they control. There are 74 ITL offices in all the regions listed above.[1] Each ITL is tasked with coordinating and rationalising individual labour inspectors' activities; regulating and supervising matters relating to labour, social legislation and income support; protecting working conditions, including the provision of civil protections; preventing, promoting, and informing actors on the correct application of labour and social security regulations; ensuring health and safety in the workplace; mediating labour disputes; and managing migration flows for labour reasons.

Inspection personnel are also part of the organisational field of workplace controls. Ministerial labour inspectors working in DTLs are joined primarily by INAIL inspectors, INPS inspectors, and Carabinieri[2] of the Labour Inspectorate Unit (NIL). The NIL depends on the General Command of the Carabinieri for labour protection. In 2009, four institutions were established, each with macro-regional responsibilities in Milan, Rome, Naples, and Palermo, which coordinate 101 NILs within each of the NIL's territorial headquarters. With the recently established Italian National Labour Inspectorate, judicial police officers' duties have been extended to inspectors of social security institutions (i.e., INAIL and INPS), thereby providing them powers that were previously the prerogative of ministerial labour inspectors. Along with the labour supervisory bodies, inspectors from the Prevention and Safety Service (SPReSAL) charged with overseeing the local health units, who are the judicial police officers who mainly deal with occupational health and safety,[3] are also

[1] No inspectorates were established in Trentino-Alto Adige and Sicily under Legislative Decree 149/2015 as these are special statute regions.

[2] Carabinieri are member of the Italian national police force, organised as a military unit and charged with maintaining public security and order as well as assisting local police.

[3] Their duties are regulated by Article 13 of Legislative Decree 81/2008.

important. Labour-related sanctions can also be ordered by the military apparatus, including the Guardia di Finanza, State Police, and Carabinieri, who can order employers to rectify any wrongdoing.

Although the pyramidal structure of control management is known, the planning and monitoring process is a bottom-up process, starting with horizontal coordination among actors at the territorial level. This is another reason why it is necessary to investigate the field. The function of labour protection and supervision is entrusted to a plurality of actors, which prompted the legislature to seek coordination among inspection services and to limit overlaps or contradictions as much as possible (Pennesi, 2004). To create coordination among the different organisations, a Central Commission for the Coordination of Supervisory Activity was established, which aims to integrate inspection policies starting from the centre and moving to interregional and then territorial levels. Members of the central commission include not only administrations that deal specifically with workplace inspections (i.e., INAIL, INPS, SPReSAL) but also administrations that deal with contextual matters, such as the Guardia di Finanza, Carabinieri, and the Internal Revenue Service. Four representatives of employers' organisations and four union representatives are needed to ensure that the direct beneficiaries of these activities are included in planning and coordination. The administrations retain autonomy in the implementation of inspection actions. The legislature also mandates quarterly consultations among the same actors at the interregional level. It also stipulates that at least six annual meetings need to be convened with the chairpersons of the Committees for Labour and Emergence of the Underside to allow for the sharing of knowledge and establishing priorities for action.

ITLs coordinate and monitor inspection functions at the territorial level, which consists of preparing statistics compiled by individual labour inspectors that are subsequently aggregated at the territorial, interregional, and central levels. Individual ITLs also have the opportunity to share their results and their decision-making strategies or interpretative uncertainties. The NIL uses materials to draft and publish circulars, operational guidelines, and answers to questions from ITLs in order to limit interpretative disputes or technical-operational criticalities related to relevant legislation or inspection activities. At the same time, in order to make the NIL's work more efficient, a series of formal collaborations have been initiated with both Italian and foreign *non-inspection bodies*. At the national level, agreements have been made with several institutions for various reasons: with the National Network of Equality Advisers to validate the resignation of mothers and fathers, with the National Council of the Order of Labour Consultants to promote joint training meetings, and with Confartigianato and the National Confederation of Craftsmen and Small and Medium Enterprises to set up joint technical tables and discuss some operational issues related to supervisory activities. Some professions are subject to ad hoc dialogue that is mandated in the agreements between the National Board of Welfare and Assistance for Biologists and the National Board of Welfare and Assistance for Physicians and Dentists. The NIL has also signed an agreement with the Carabinieri Corps to counter the criminal phenomena related to the exploitation of labour, illegal employment, and compliance with safety conditions. Collaboration with the Guardia di Finanza has also been formalised, with particular reference to combating undeclared work, tax evasion, and failure to implement health and safety regulations.

The organisational field of workplace controls is not only structured at the national level as it is also affected by the European Parliament and European Union (EU) directives that emphasise the need for strong and coordinated prevention and inspection activities as well as the various international organisations that set standards and build scientific knowledge on labour irregularity issues such as the International Labour Organization (ILO), all of which results in countries jointly contributing to shared projects.[4] Moreover, popularisers, opinion makers, individual policy-makers, and the scientific community are also very important in building knowledge and expertise on labour issues in the organisational field of workplace controls. This is the *epistemic community* (Bertozzi & Bonoli, 2002; Borghi & Rizza, 2006).

[4] These include the international projects and initiatives in which NIL has participated in recent years: The Prevention of and Fight against Crime in 2008 and 2009, which was created to combat human trafficking for labour exploitation; the Special Action Program to combat forced labour in 2010, which was formed to counteract new forms of slavery; the Cooperation for a European Network against Undeclared Work in 2010, which focused on ensuring the cooperation of inspection services; the EMPOWER, Exchange of Experiences and Implementation of Actions for Posted Workers in 2010, which aimed to align strategies to counteract posted labour; the Convergence of Inspectorates Building a European Level Enforcement System in 2011, which was related to posted labour in Europe and work performance involving transnational implications; and the Road Transport Sector and Posting of Workers in 2012, which was concerned with posted labour in the transport sector.

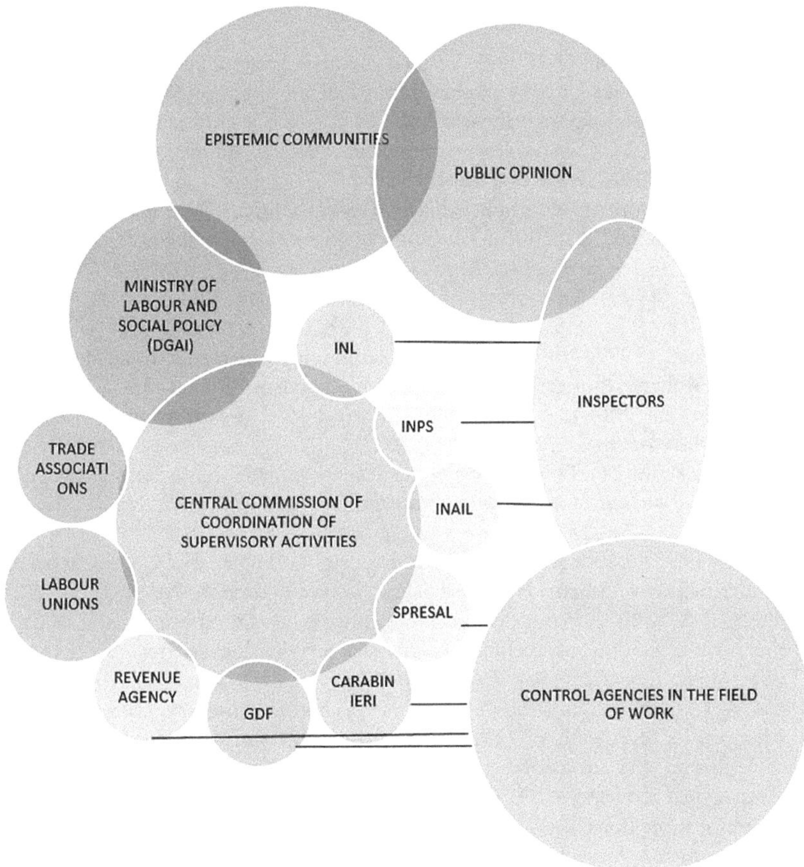

Fig. 2.1 The actors in the organisational field of workplace controls. (Source: Author elaboration)

These individual and institutional and non-institutional actors thus contribute, through recursive interactions, to constructing a model of intervention for serious forms of work irregularity (Fig. 2.1).

References

Bertozzi, F., & Bonoli, G. (2002). Verso una convergenza delle politiche nazionali per l'occupazione? La costruzione di un modello europeo attraverso il metodo di coordinamento aperto. *Rivista italiana di politiche pubbliche, 3*, 31–57.

Bonazzi, G. (2002). *Come studiare le organizzazioni*. Il Mulino.

Bonazzi, G. (2004). Teorie dell'impresa e ricerca sociologica: prospettive e problemi di un incontro. *Rassegna Italiana di Sociologia, 2*, 179–212.

Borghi, V., & Rizza, R. (2006). *L'organizzazione sociale del lavoro. Lo statuto del lavoro e le sue trasformazioni*. Mondadori.

Bourdieu, P. (1999). Une révolution conservatrice dans l'édition'. *Actes de la Recherche en Sciences Sociales, 126*(127), 3–28.

Brodkin, E. Z. (1997). Inside the welfare contract: Discretion and accountability in state welfare administration. *Social Service Review, 71*(1), 1–33.

Brodkin, E. Z. (2008). Accountability in street-level organizations. *Journal of Public Administration, 31*(3), 317–336.

Brodkin, E. Z. (2011). Policy work: Street-level organizations under new managerialism. *Journal of Public Administration Research and Theory, 21*(suppl_2), 253–277.

Chan, A. (1998). Labor standards and human rights: The case of Chinese workers under market socialism. *Human Rights Quarterly, 20*, 886–901.

Colyvas, J. A. (2007). From divergent meanings to common practices: The early institutionalization of technology transfer in the life sciences at Stanford University. *Research Policy, 36*(4), 456–476.

Davis, K. C. (1969). *Discretionary justice: A preliminary inquiry*. LSU Press.

DiMaggio, P., & Powell, W. (1983). The Iron Cage Revisited: Institutional isomorphism and collective rationality in organizational fields. *American Sociological Review, 48*, 147–160.

DiMaggio, P., & Powell, W. (Eds.). (1991). *The new institutionalism in organizational analysis*. University of Chicago Press.

Dixon, J., Levine, M., Reicher, S., & Durrheim, K. (2012). Beyond prejudice: Are negative evaluations the problem and is getting us to like one another more the solution? *Behavioral and Brain Sciences, 35*(6), 411–425.

Dubois, V. (2010). *The bureaucrat and the poor: Encounters in French welfare offices*. Routledge.

Dworkin, R. (1978). *Taking rights seriously*. Duckworth.

Ellis, K. (2011). 'Street-level bureaucracy' revisited: The changing face of frontline discretion in adult social care in England. *Social Policy & Administration, 45*(3), 221–244.

Evans, T. (2016). *Professional discretion in welfare services: Beyond street-level bureaucracy*. Routledge.

Evans, T., & Harris, J. (2004). Street-level bureaucracy, social work and the (exaggerated) death of discretion. *British Journal of Social Work, 34*(6), 871–895.
Fineman, S. (1998). Street-level bureaucrats and the social construction of environmental control. *Organization Studies, 19*(6), 953–974.
Freidson, E. (1970). The social organization of illness. In M. Bury & J. Gabe (Eds.), *The sociology of health and illness. A reader* (pp. 177–184). Routledge.
Giddens, A. (1984). *The constitution of society: Outline of the theory of structuration*. University of California Press.
Gilboy, J. A. (1992). Penetrability of administrative system: Political casework and immigration inspections. *Law & Society Review, 26*, 273.
Goosensen, H. R. (2021). *Inzicht in de praktijk van het toezicht: Een empirisch onderzoek naar het verloop van operationele inspectieprocessen in de luchtvaart en zeevaart* (Doctoral dissertation, Delft University of Technology).
Goosensen, H. R., & van der Voort, H. G. (2009). Risk based oversight: The story of street-level inspectors. In *Annual meeting of the Law and Society Association (LSA)* (pp. 1–18). Blackwell.
Ham, C., & Hill, M. (1986). *Introduzione all'analisi delle politiche pubbliche*. Il Mulino.
Hawkins, K. (1992). The use of legal discretion: Perspectives from law and social science. In K. Hawkins (Ed.), *The uses of discretion* (p. 11). Clarendon Press.
Hill, M. (1969). The exercise of discretion in the National Assistance Board. *Public Administration, 47*(1), 75–90.
Hupe, P. (2013). Dimensions of discretion: Specifying the object of street-level bureaucracy research. *Der Moderne Staat, 6*, 425–440.
Hupe, P. (Ed.). (2019). *Research handbook on street-level bureaucracy*. Edward Elgar Publishing.
Hupe, P., & Hill, M. (2007). Street-level bureaucracy and public accountability. *Public Administration, 85*(2), 279–299.
Kagan, J. (1997). Temperament and the reactions to unfamiliarity. *Child Development, 68*(1), 139–143.
Kazepov, Y., & Barberis, E. (2012). Social assistance governance in Europe. Towards a multi-level perspective. In I. Marx & K. Nelson (Eds.), *Minimum income protection in flux*. Palgrave Macmillan.
Kelly, M. (1994). Theories of justice and street-level discretion. *Journal of Public Administration Research &Theory, 4*(2), 119–140.
Lipsky, M. (1980). *Street level bureaucracy. Dilemmas of the individual in public services*. Russell Sage Foundation.
Lipsky, M. (2010). *Street level bureaucracy. Dilemmas of the individual in public services* 30th Anniversary Expanded Edition. Russell Sage Foundation.
Loyens, K. (2015). Law enforcement and policy alienation—Coping by labour inspectors and federal police officers. In P. Hupe, M. Hill, & A. Buffat (Eds.), *Understanding street level bureaucracy*. Bristol Policy Press.

Loyens, K. (2016). How police detectives deal with policy alienation in the investigation of human exploitation crimes. In R. J. Burke (Ed.), *Stress in policing: Sources, consequences and interventions.* Routledge.

Loyens, K., & Paraciani, R. (2023). Who is the ("ideal") victim of labor exploitation? Two qualitative vignette studies on labor inspectors' discretion. *The Sociological Quarterly, 64*(1), 27–45.

May, P. J., & Wood, R. S. (2003). At the regulatory front lines: Inspectors' enforcement styles and regulatory compliance. *Journal of Public Administration Research and Theory, 13*(2), 117–139.

Maynard-Moody, S. W., & Musheno, M. C. (2003). *Cops, teachers, counselors: Stories from the front lines of public service.* University of Michigan Press.

Merton, R. K. (1940). Fact and factitiousness in ethnic opinionnaires. *American Sociological Review, 5*(1), 13–28.

Meyer, J. W., & Rowan, B. (1977). Institutionalized organizations: Formal structure as myth and ceremony. *American Journal of Sociology, 83*(2), 340–363.

Meyers, M. K., & Vorsanger, S. (2003). Street-level bureaucrats and the implementation of public policy. In B. G. Peters & J. Pierre (Eds.), *Handbook of public administration* (pp. 245–254). Sage.

Miller, G. A. (1967). Professionals in bureaucracy: Alienation among industrial scientists and engineers. *American Sociological Review, 32*(5), 755–768.

Nielsen, V. L. (2006). Are street-level bureaucrats compelled or enticed to cope? *Public Administration, 84*(4), 861–889.

Paraciani, R., & Saruis, T. (2019). When the law is not enough: Caseworkers' ideas of justice in practices. *Sociologia del Lavoro, 152*, 163–182.

Paraciani, R., & Rizza, R. (2021). When the workplace is the home: Labour inspectors' discretionary power in the field of domestic work – an institutional analysis. *Journal of Public Policy, 41*(1), 1–16.

Pennesi, P. (2004). La riforma dei servizi ispettivi. In M. Tiraboschi (Ed.), *La riforma Biagi del mercato del lavoro: Prime interpretazioni e proposte di lettura del d.lgs. 10 settembre 2003, n. 276. Il diritto transitorio e i tempi della riforma*, Giuffrè.

Piore, M. J., & Schrank, A. (2008). Toward managed flexibility: The revival of labour inspection in the Latin world. *International Labour Review, 147*(1), 1–23.

Piore, M. J., & Schrank, A. (2018). *Root-cause regulation: Protecting work and workers in the twenty-first century.* Harvard University Press.

Prottas, J. M. (1979). *People processing: The street-level bureaucrat in public service bureaucracies.* Lexington Books.

Raaphorst, N. (2018). How to prove how to interpret and what to do? Uncertainty experiences of street-level tax officials. *Public Management Review, 20*(4), 485–502.

Raaphorst, N., & Loyens, K. (2020). From poker games to kitchen tables: How social dynamics affect frontline decision making. *Administration & Society, 52*(1), 31–56.

Raspanti, D., & Saruis, T. (2022). Trapped into reverse asymmetry: Public employment services dealing with employers. *Journal of Social Policy, 51*(1), 173–190.
Reiss, A. J. (1984). Selecting strategies of social control over organizational life. In K. Hawkins & J. Thomas (Eds.), *Enforcing regulation* (pp. 23–35). KluwerNijhoff Publishing.
Rice, D. (2013). Street-level bureaucrats and the welfare state: Toward a micro-institutionalist theory of policy implementation. *Administration & Society, 45*(9), 1038–1062.
Rice, D. (2019). Adopting an institutional view in street-level bureaucracy research. In P. Hupe (Ed.), *Research handbook on street-level bureaucracy* (pp. 70–85). Edward Elgar Publishing.
Ricucci, N. (2005). Street-level bureaucrat and intrastate variation in the implementation of temporary assistance for needy families policies. *Journal of Public Administration, 15*, 89–111.
Saruis, T. (2015). *Gli operatori sociali nel nuovo welfare: tra discrezionalità e responsabilità*. Carocci editore.
Schrank, A., & Piore, M. J. (2007). *Norms, regulations and labor standards in Central America*. ECLAC.
Scott, W. R. (1997). *Institutions and organizations*. Sage.
Smith, R. P. (1981 [1979]). *Book reviews: Using research in organizations: A guide to successful application*. Jack Rothman, Sage Publications.
Van Berkel, R., & Knies, E. (2018). The frontline delivery of activation: Workers' preferences and their antecedents. *European Journal of Social Work, 21*(4), 602–615.
Van de Walle, S., & Raaphorst, N. (Eds.). (2019). *Inspectors and enforcement at the front line of government*. Palgrave Macmillan.
Vinzant, J., & Crothers, L. (1998). *Street-level leader-ship: Discretion and legitimacy in front-line public service*. Georgetown University Press.
Walker, R. B. (1993). *Inside/outside: International relations as political theory*. Cambridge University Press.
Watkins-Hayes, C. (2013). The micro dynamics of support seeking: The social and economic utility of institutional ties for HIV-positive women. *The ANNALS of the American Academy of Political and Social Science, 647*(1), 83–101.
Wiering, M. A. (1999). *Explorations in efficient reinforcement learning* (Doctoral dissertation, University of Amsterdam).
Winter, S. G. (2003). Understanding dynamic capabilities. *Strategic Management Journal, 24*(10), 991–995.
Zucker, L. G. (1987). Institutional theories of organization. *Annual Review of Sociology, 13*, 443–464.

CHAPTER 3

An Italian Case Study: Labour Inspectors Dealing with Labour Exploitation

Abstract This chapter centres on the Italian context. The regulatory ambiguity surrounding the phenomenon of labour exploitation in Italy is presented. After this, the ways in which the exploitation is classified as "severe," which falls under criminal jurisdiction, or "non-severe," which is considered part of labour law jurisdiction, are discussed. The reference legislation is so vague that it is difficult to apply. Therefore, labour inspectors' discretion is a fundamental work tool. Through documentary analysis, the inspectors' powers and professional duties as well as the ways in which they have changed over time are detailed. The last section uses a purely neo-institutionalist perspective to reinterpret labour inspectors' main organisational and professional transformations that occur through coercive, mimetic, and normative isomorphic pressures.

Keywords Labour exploitation • Work irregularities • Italian Labour Inspectorate • Isomorphism

R. Paraciani, *Labour Inspectors in Italy*,
https://doi.org/10.1007/978-3-031-37997-0_3

3.1 Discretion and Work Irregularities: The Fine Line Between Severe and Non-severe Labour Exploitation

In Italy, there is no clear, unambiguous, and agreed-upon definition of what is meant by "labour exploitation." If the term "exploitation" is isolated, there are two meanings: According to a neutral perspective, "exploitation" means using or taking advantage of resources, skills, and opportunities, while another perspective states that exploitation occurs when one seeks to gain an unjustified advantage at the expense of another person. The demarcation between the two definitions is far from clear. Wertheimer refers to the concept of "fairness of transactions" (Wertheimer, 1996, p. 14) to emphasise that exploitation occurs when there is an exchange that is not beneficial to both parties and unfair to one of them, which is generally the weaker party. Steiner et al. (1984) define this concept by identifying three types of transactions between people: gift, exchange, and theft. Gift and theft are both one-sided transactions, while exchange is a bilateral transaction in that it is a quid pro quo. Exchange degenerates into exploitation when the transfer is of unequal value (defined as non-altruistic). It is not the agents' motivation that gives rise to non-altruistic bilateral transactions but rather the circumstances within which these transactions take place. Steiner and colleagues added an additional piece of information to this definition: The non-altruistic transaction must also involve the violation of others' rights. Moreover, Sensat (1984) states that exploitation occurs when someone is used as a medium. According to this perspective, exploitation takes the form of using a person for a particular purpose in ways that are contrary to the nature or will of the person being used. The use of a person is defined as wrong or improper when that person is vulnerable and their being used benefits other people, usually the exploiter (Wood, 1995). What differentiates exploitation from abuse and, thus, in the case at hand, what differentiates exploitative labour from forms of forced labour or servitude is both parties deriving some benefit from the situation preceding the exploitative relationship (Del Bò, 2004). In this case, a person who accepts an exploitative labour relationship is promised the remuneration they need, even if it is less than what they would obtain under regular conditions, but they cannot access the remuneration.

Irregularities in labour matters can take different forms and vary in intensity. Additionally, they can be administrative, contributory, or economic in nature (Buffa et al., 2017). The labour relationship can be grey, which means that the relationship is declared but it is not in compliance with the rules, or black, which means that it is completely formalised. Included in the definition of labour exploitation are situations of imbalance in the exchange of benefits between labour and wages or situations that infringe upon the rights of the weaker party. This phenomenon manifests in different forms that can be placed along a continuum of which one extreme (in Fig. 3.1: the top of the pyramid) is characterised by real forms of abuse and slavery, while the other side represents relatively less serious forms of exploitation that do not constitute criminal offences (European Union Agency for Fundamental Rights, FRA, 2015).

The present research considers work irregularity cases that border the first and second rungs of the pyramid, and it aims to determine an understanding of the ways in which (i.e., organisational or individual) a case of labour exploitation is defined as severe or non-severe, thus placing them in the first or second rung of the pyramid (see Fig. 3.1), and what are the criteria for these demarcations.

Labour inspectors find themselves making decisions on how to resolve different work irregularities at different times. This involves three elements: the complaints desk; the dispute-settlement procedure room; and the labour inspectors' offices in which the *back-office* work occurs. The complaints desk is where the worker files a complaint and where the labour

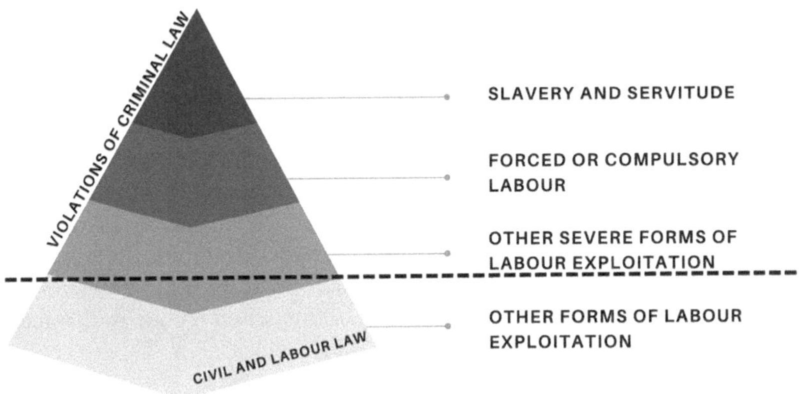

Fig. 3.1 Pyramid of labour exploitation. (Source: FRA, 2015, author elaboration)

inspector decides whether to investigate the complaint and determine an administrative solution or to not open the case at all. In dispute-settlement procedures, the possibility provided by Legislative Decree 124/2004 to find an administrative solution for the resolution of wage and contribution conflicts is materialised. This step precedes inspections, which take place only in the event of a failure to reach an agreement between the worker and the employer. The labour inspector here is a third, impartial figure who, based on a worker's statements, undertakes to find the best possible solution for both parties. By resolving the dispute at this stage, the employer is exempt from any kind of penalty. The inspector can decide whether to encourage an economic solution between the parties or to prevent conciliation. During the investigation stage, labour inspectors decide how to gather information about the case and whether or not to make the workplace inspection at all. Dilemmas in these interventions mainly comprise labour inspectors not being able to investigate all cases that are presented to them due to insufficient resources. Moreover, in some situations, there are regulatory overlaps for which the inspector's interpretive action is necessary.

From a legal perspective, labour exploitation is regulated by Article 603bis of the Penal Code,[1] reformulated by Legal Decree 199/2016. It punishes the employer who subjects workers to exploitative conditions and takes advantage of their state of need. The Italian and EU legislature refrain from providing a precise definition of "exploitation" or the state in which workers need to be in order for them to be taken advantage of for the crime to exist. Instead, it merely provides some legal indices of evidence of exploitation, upon which the "needle of the scales" is based (Piva, 2017). Under the 2016 reformulation of this article, labour exploitation can materialise even without the occurrence of illegal labour brokering, thereby making employers responsible by including them among the active subjects of the crime. Legal Decree 199/2016 intends to simplify the previous version of Article 603bis, which was practically inapplicable, by more readily classifying the conduct that limits the ability to resist prevarication, thereby providing greater protection for the victims of exploitation. Labour exploitation, then, occurs when labour is characterised by one or more of the following conditions:

[1] Italian Criminal Code, Book II, Title XII, Chapter III, Section I, Article 603a, "Illegal intermediation and exploitation of labour."

1. Repeated payment of wages that are blatantly different from what is stipulated in national collective agreements;
2. Repeated violations related to working hours, expectations, and vacations;
3. Lack of compliance with workplace safety and hygiene regulations; and
4. Degrading working conditions, surveillance methods, or housing situations.

This clarifies how this attempt at simplification resulted in a very broad and general wording of the rule, which made it difficult to apply Article 603a (Piva, 2017).

Until now, research on labour exploitation has focused on human trafficking (Ciconte & Romani, 2002; Carchedi, 2010; Nocifora, 2014; Chuang, 2014), which is the recruitment, transportation, and transfer of people through coercion and abusing their vulnerability for the purpose of exploitation, including prostitution and other forms of sex work, forced labour, slavery or similar conditions, servitude, and organ harvesting. Another strand of research has sought to understand the role of male and female workers in determining and negotiating their exploitation conditions (i.e., Rovelli, 2008; Sacchetto, 2009; Perrotta, 2014; Leogrande, 2016; Piro, 2021). These studies were carried out on construction sites and in the agriculture, domestic labour, and tourism sectors.

The analysis proposed here adopts a different perspective by using the street-level bureaucrat to determine how the definition of severe labour exploitation is derived and which processes are used in labour inspectors' operational practices. In summary, the ways in which these practitioners give form and substance to labour exploitation and thus contribute to its social construction is investigated (Berger & Luckmann, 1967). In this framework, the institutional context in which inspectors' practices occur plays an essential role, which is defined as the organisational field of workplace controls herein.

3.2 The Organisational Transformations of the Italian National Labour Inspectorate

The Italian National Labour Inspectorate has recently seen transformations. A brief reconstruction of the most recent history aimed to capture the changes in this organisation, thereby taking up the challenge posed by Scott (2008): to give space to the process that led to the choice of an organisational form in order to place it in relation to its environment. The late nineteenth century saw the introduction of a professional figure whose skills in workplace supervision can be considered anticipatory of those of labour inspectors: the inspector of industry and industrial teaching within the Ministry of Agriculture, Industry, and Commerce. A host of inspectors and engineers for mines, quarries, and peat bogs was established, but it was composed of a few inspectors from industries with different functions (Dragoni, 1904). This organised supervisory apparatus was not sufficient for the enforcement of legislation to protect women and children especially, and supervisory action was opposed by industrialists (Zucchetti et al., 2001). The need for a supervisory system capable of regulating the protection of male and female workers and safeguarding them was therefore evident. The impetus for the creation of this organisation came from France and the French-Italian convention signed in Rome in order to protect domestic workers who worked abroad through the organisation of a state-regulated supervisory service. Under Legal Decree 547/1904, the Italian government agreed to establish an inspection service operating under the state that is capable of enforcing laws in a manner similar to the French inspection service, declaring laws that protect women and minors to be its main focus. This represents the first of several attempts to enact state-level enforcement of legislation that was targeted towards circumventing the exploitation and oppression of male and female workers.

The founding act of the *Ispettorato dell'Industria e del Lavoro* in Italy is represented by Legal Decree 1361/1912, and it delimited the National Labour Inspectorate's competencies and powers by outlining its compulsory functions (e.g., supervision of the application of labour regulations and monitoring of labour problems) and optional functions (e.g., peaceful settlement of labour disputes when requested by the parties). Inspectors were also given their most characteristic attributes: visiting workplaces at any time of the day or night and being able to identify those who refused to obey them as criminal. The first labour inspectorate was located within the Ministry of Agriculture, Industry, and Trade. Under this corporative regime, the labour inspectorate ensured discipline in terms of labour police duties and powers, but it changed its name to the Inspectorate of Corporations (r.d. 2183/1929). With the collapse of fascism, the Ministry of Labour was established (r.d. 377/1945), and Italy became a republic founded on labour. Article 1 of the Constitutional Charter, in fact, elevates labour as the foundation of the state's structure. Therefore, protecting this pillar is essential for guaranteeing the principle of effective freedom and concrete equality. The republic, with this article, is committed to protecting labour in all its forms and applications, with preferential protection being afforded to workers (Zagrebelsky, 2013).

Meanwhile, on the international level, the ILO adopted an extensive and dense convention on labour inspections. The *Labour Inspection Convention* sets out the guiding principles in terms of which member states must comply with the organisation of national labour inspection services. The ILO proposed a threefold operational framework in that it was designed to ensure the enforcement of labour law provisions, to provide information and technical advice to employers and workers, and to bring any deficiencies or abuses to the attention of the authorities (C81/1947). The convention, while covering trade and industry, is an important landmark in labour inspection.

In 1953, Law 429 reorganised the labour inspectorate, which was reintroduced and regulated in 1955 due to the Presidential Decree 520 on central and peripheral reorganisation of the Ministry of Labour and Social Security. Chapter II of the legislation (Art. 6–Art. 21) regulates the activities of the National Labour Inspectorate, whose activities occur on several levels due to regional and provincial offices, the activities of which are organised and monitored by the headquarters. Article 7 specifies the tasks of the National Labour Inspectorate, which includes supervising the execution of labour and social security laws wherever wage labour is performed with the legal exceptions, supervising the regularity of collective labour agreements, and ensuring social security, welfare, and sanitation activities to benefit workers. The National Labour Inspectorate must follow the instructions of the ministry on which it depends for the detection of working conditions within enterprises. Likewise, it must monitor the number, causes, and consequences of workplace accidents, study labour regulations, collect all news and information on working conditions nationwide, and conduct surveys, investigations, and inquiries. This normative device elevates labour inspectors to judicial police officers, assigning them the power of inspection access. They can, in fact, visit "in any part, at any hour of the day or night, laboratories, factories, construction sites, dormitories, and refectories attached to establishments; they shall refrain from visiting premises attached to workplaces not directly or indirectly connected with the operation of the business, unless they have well-founded suspicions that they serve to carry out or conceal violations of the law" (Art. 8 DPR 520/1955).

In the 1950s, labour protection was the community's and the Italian legislature's focus, which included safety and hygiene in the workplace. In particular, the right to safety became one of the main rights of workers that was considered a true paradigm and led to the concept of prevention being introduced. Presidential Decree 547/1955 focused on prevention in general, and it was followed by Presidential Decree 303/1956, which centred around the subject of hygiene in the workplace. Both of these constituted an initial attempt in this direction, but they suffered several criticisms, including their overly general statements and overly technical aims, the focus of which was on the technical-objective control of safety devices and environmental suitability conditions, thereby neglecting the relationship between risk factors and the worker and technological changes, which are far more rapid than regulatory ones. Within a broader process of democratisation in Italy in the 1970s, the Workers' Statute outlined the importance of protecting healthy workplaces (Rizza & Sansavini, 2013), and Legal Decree 833/1978 extended labour inspectors' typical warning powers to local health units.

The 1990s represented a turning point for the creation and sedimentation of a culture of prevention in areas as diverse as work settings. Community thrusts enshrined the culture of prevention as an unbreakable principle that national legislature must implement through national laws that pursue prevention through corporate reorganisation. In fact, the novelty of Community Directive 89/391/EEC lies not so much in the introduction of a new culture of prevention as in a new means of pursuing it, which was translated into Italian law in the form of Legislative Decree 626/1994, which makes companies responsible for their choices about the organisation of work and also involves the worker in this process, giving them the right to be trained and informed on the subject of safety and health in the workplace. Italian legislation also extends these measures to all sectors of activity, including the service sector and public administrations. In the same time frame, the National Labour Inspectorate also underwent transformations: With Ministerial Decree 687/1996, in line with the decentralisation that swept the public sector starting with the health sector, the National Labour Inspectorate was reorganised at the territorial level, thereby losing its functional autonomy and becoming a service of the Provincial Labour Directorate, which is divided into Territorial Directorates. In 2004, there was a major reorganisation of supervisory responsibilities. Legislative Decree 124/2004 followed in the wake of the liberalisation present in the Biagi Law (Legislative Decree 276/2003), which can be summarised as rationalisation, ordering, and coordination as well as responding to the demand for quality and effectiveness in inspections in order to prevent abuse and to sanction substantial irregularities (Gualmini & Rizza, 2013). The main novelties include the introduction of totally new powers for labour inspectors, including the ascertainment warning and the dispute-settlement procedures, which is the subject of the following in-depth study. With the Directive 18/2008, the Ministry Sacconi reaffirmed the preventive and promotional philosophy of the reformed supervisory activity and, in line with international institutional thrusts and public sector reform, inspection action was oriented according to the criteria of intervention planning and the efficiency, effectiveness, and economic principles in organisational action. Labour inspectors must be credible and authoritative as they need to assume a decisive role in the proper functioning of the system of control on the ground and implementation of local, national, EU, and international policies. This directive, in conjunction with the guiding principles of Legal Decree 124/2004, requalified the idea of the inspector, who is called upon to contribute actively to the governance and control of the labour market in line with the relevant ILO directives. Additionally, the Sacconi directive also established indicators that can be used to measure the effectiveness of inspection action within a provincial territory. Additionally, in order to achieve a standard of efficiency, it is essential to coordinate preventive action, starting from the centre. The achievement of this goal will depend not only on the training, professionalism, and competence of inspectors but also on "the ability to interpret the institutional role of the inspector in a modern and effective way" (Directive 18/2008 2). The latest reformation inspired by Legal Decree 124/2004 is Legal Decree 183/2010, which is the labour connection that led to a rewriting of Article 13 of Legal Decree 124/2004 to make the objectives of simplification and transparency more explicit, clarify the contents of inspection reports, and strengthen the use of one-on-one conciliation. Moreover, Legal Decree 149/2015 for the rationalisation and simplification of inspection activities in the field of labour and social legislation will allow the National Labour Inspectorate to undergo a final transformation. This 2015 Legal Decree bases its rationale in the Jobs Act, the main objective of which is to rationalise public spending and simplify labour relations and labour inspection. The new National Labour Inspectorate was created from this framework: a single labour inspection agency that integrates the inspection services of the Ministry of Labour and Social Policy, INPS, and INAIL for improved coordination of activities while avoiding overlaps.

3.3 Institutional Isomorphism and Inspection Activities

The regulatory and organisational changes summarised so far have had a profoundly changed inspection activities. Legislative processes and organisational choices at the EU and national levels have highlighted a general trend towards simplification. However, there has been a more recent move towards standardising decision-making processes, undertaking investigations, and conducting inspections. The stated aim is to reduce the differences in action between one territorial inspectorate office and another or, more specifically, between one labour inspector and another. This simplification has led to labour supervisory bodies' tasks being unified, which has translated into procedures being streamlined. This streamlining has also resulted in the ministerial identification of priority areas for action, including combating undeclared labour and enforcing safety regulations in the workplace.

In terms of the organisational field of workplace controls, it is possible to identify certain change trends that can be read through the lens of isomorphism processes. The strengthening of relationships among the various actors that are part of the organisational field of workplace controls has resulted in definite changes. The first recognisable form of isomorphism is coercive, which is the result of a formal reorganisation of the organisational arrangements of workplace controls. The pressures come from the national legislature, the Ministry of Labour and Social Policy, and international bodies, such as the EU legislature and the ILO. These pressures result in two main actions:

1. The simplification of the organisation of controls; and
2. The introduction of measures to monitor the effectiveness and efficiency of inspection activities.

These pressures institutionalise organisational procedures largely inspired by the principles of *New Public Management* (NPM), which proposes the same solutions to different contexts: modernisation and efficiency (Hood, 1991). The literature on NPM is vast (Osborne & Gaebler, 1993) and contains a common understanding of the general elements that comprise the basis of NPM actions and reforms (McLaughlin et al., 2001). First, at the organisational level, there is a redistribution of responsibilities and a reduction of the traditional hierarchy. In terms of managerial choices, planning is conducted through setting objectives and is based on efficiency. Finally, for budget management, practices typical of the private sector are implemented within the public sector: Quantity becomes the key to measuring individual and organisational progress and understanding the ways in which to allocate ever-shrinking budgets (Pollitt, 2007). In NPM, the emphasis is not on processes but on efficiency, which is measured through outputs and accountability processes that are determined through targets, success indicators, and performance measurement criteria (Fatemi & Behmanesh, 2012). The broad purpose is to "replace the supposed inefficiency of hierarchical bureaucracy with the supposed efficiency of markets" (Power, 2010, p. 61). In pursuit of this purpose that is, for all intents and purposes, a rationalised myth, the National Labour Inspectorate incorporates organisational modes in line with the socially legitimised belief in the superiority of business organisation over bureaucratic organisation because it is more oriented towards the achievement of efficiency that is measured through the results obtained.

Consequently, accounting for the inspections conducted and cases resolved is required as this is as the supreme yardstick of efficiency. To achieve this, there is a move towards gradually decriminalising labour offences. Until Legal Decree 689/1981 was enacted, the National Labour Inspectorate was limited to ascertaining labour and social security violations. However, since 1981, it has also had the power to dispense the relevant penalties. There was a wave of decriminalisation that occurred due to Legal Decree 8/2016, which transformed labour and social security offences from criminal to administrative offences and identified specific sanction measures. Thus, on the one hand, the declared seriousness of labour offences decreased, and on the other hand, the number of cases that labour inspectors can resolve without going through a court of law increased. However, this decree increases the number of cases that territorial offices have to handle and also contributes, in the face of reduced resources, to the introduction of practices aimed at simplifying procedures for handling work irregularity cases. Additionally, performance monitoring and streamlining of procedures, especially those that arise from the introduction of dispute-settlement procedures, are becoming increasingly pressing. In particular, preventive conciliatory tools, the use of which is discretionary, are now preferred over repressive action because of both the expansion of the INL's scope of intervention and because the mechanism allows for a large number of requests for action to be completed quickly, thereby avoiding unnecessary backlogs in public offices that would slow down timely intervention by the public body. Thus, dispute-settlement procedures are the most effective tool for resolving labour disputes.

There are also other forms of pressure leading to organisational changes based on processes of isomorphism, the origin of which can be traced to the increase in the number of offences that need to be sanctioned and the complexity of labour relations, which is a source of increasing uncertainty in the inspection field. Pressures can then be identified that lead to mimetic isomorphism, which is aimed at resolving uncertainties and results in the sharing of inspection guidelines among INL territorial offices in the form of circulars and opinions. The increased complexity is being responded to in an increasingly standardised way, with one imperative: "getting back on track" and "accountability" in effective operations that involves governance reverting to dependence on the centre. This affirms the principle of accountability, which is a process through which the National Labour Inspectorate must demonstrate the consistency of its actions through accountability mechanisms in line with the established objectives and the resources at its disposal, as is the case for other public administrations (Moini, 2015). A practice created in response to demands for transparency in terms of public administration in order to regain social legitimacy can be used to demonstrate how resources are used to taxpayers. These are changes that led to the introduction of performance evaluation and inspection outcomes.

There is also a tendency towards implementing organisational change that is influenced by external pressures in the field under consideration. This includes the urge to conform that stems, in this case, from an awareness of the superiority of certain solutions, and it leads to normative processes of isomorphism (DiMaggio & Powell, 1983), which are intimately linked to the changes that the inspector profession has undergone in recent decades. One trend concerns the increased number of educational qualifications needed to enter the profession (i.e., a master's degree) and channelling a profession using paths hegemonised by legal or economic disciplines. An education path that standardises the knowledge held by inspectors who are appropriately trained in clearly oriented settings is therefore needed. Another trend relates to training provided within the organisation that aims to increase the harmonisation between practices and skills.

References

Berger, P. L., & Luckmann, T. (1967). *The social construction of reality. A treatise in the sociology of knowledge.* Anchor Books Edition.

Buffa, F., Gadaleta, L., & Riverso, R. (2017). *Sfruttamento lavorativo.* Key Editore.

Carchedi, F. (Ed.). (2010). *Schiavitù di ritorno: il fenomeno del lavoro gravemente sfruttato: le vittime, i servizi di protezione, i percorsi di uscita, il quadro normativo.* Maggioli editore.

Chuang, J. A. (2014). Exploitation creep and the unmaking of human trafficking law. *American Journal of International Law, 108*(4), 609–649.

Ciconte, E., & Romani, P. (2002). *Le nuove schiavitù: il traffico degli esseri umani nell'Italia del XXI secolo.* Editori riuniti.

Del Bò, C. (2004). *Un reddito per tutti: un'introduzione al basic income.* Ibis.

DiMaggio, P., & Powell, W. (1983). The Iron Cage Revisited: Institutional isomorphism and collective rationality in organizational fields. *American Sociological Review, 48*, 147–160.

Dragoni, C. (1904). Sull'istituzione di un ispettorato del lavoro. *Giornale degli Economisti, 19*(15), 309–317.

Fatemi, M., & Behmanesh, M. R. (2012). New public management approach and accountability. *International Journal of Management, Economics and Social Sciences (IJMESS), 1*(2), 42–49.

FRA. (2015), *Severe labour exploitation: Workers moving within or into the European Union: States' obligations and victims' rights.* Vienna.

Gualmini, E., & Rizza, R. (2013). *Le politiche del lavoro.* Il Mulino.

Hood, C. (1991). A public management for all seasons? *Public Administration, 69*(1), 3–19.

Leogrande, A. (2016). Il caporalato e le nuove schiavitù. *Parolechiave, 24*(1), 103–108.

McLaughlin, E., Muncie, J., & Hughes, G. (2001). The permanent revolution: New Labour, new public management and the modernization of criminal justice. *Criminal Justice, 1*(3), 301–318.

Moini, G. (Ed.) (2015), *Neoliberismi e azione pubblica: Il caso italiano*, Roma: Ediesse.

Nocifora, E. (2014). *Quasi schiavi.* Maggioli Editore.

Osborne, D., & Gaebler, T. (1993). *Reinventing government: The five strategies for reinventing government.* Plume.
Perrotta, D. (2014). Vecchi e nuovi mediatori. Storia, geografia ed etnografia del caporalato in agricoltura. *Meridiana*, 193–220.
Piro, V. (2021). *Migrant farmworkers in 'plastic factories': Investigating work-life struggles.* Palgrave Macmillan.
Piva, D. (2017). *I limiti dell'intervento penale sul caporalato come sistema (e non condotta) di produzione: brevi note a margine della legge n. 199/2016*, 184–196.
Pollitt, C. (2007). The new public management: An overview of its current status. *Administratie Si Management Public, 8*, 110.
Power, M. (2010). *La società dei controlli.* Edizioni di comunità.
Rizza, R., & Sansavini, M. (2013). Pragmatiche della sicurezza sul lavoro fra pratiche organizzative e discorsi. *Sociologia del Lavoro, 130*, 103–120.
Rovelli, C. (2008). Loop quantum gravity. *Living Reviews in Relativity, 11*(1), 5.
Sacchetto, D. (2009). *Fabbriche galleggianti: solitudine e sfruttamento dei nuovi marinai.* Editoriale Jaca Book.
Scott, W. R. (2008). Lords of the dance: Professionals as institutional agents. *Organization Studies, 29*(2), 219–238.
Sensat, J. (1984). *Exploitation.* Nous, 21–38.
Steiner, J. R., Briggs, T. L., & Gross, G. M. (1984). Emerging social work traditions, profession building, and curriculum policy statements. *Journal of Education for Social Work, 20*(1), 23–31.
Wertheimer, A. (1996). Remarks on coercion and exploitation. *Denv. UL Rev, 74*, 889.
Wood, A. W. (1995). Exploitation. *Social Philosophy And Policy, 12*(2), 136–158.
Zagrebelsky, G. (2013). *Fondata sul lavoro. La solitudine dell'articolo 1.* Einaudi.
Zucchetti, R., Capone, M., & Carra, A. (2001). *Manuale di ispezione sulla sicurezza del lavoro.* Maggioli.

CHAPTER 4

Rooms of Discretion: Evidence from the Field

Abstract This chapter describes the local office observed and the "rooms of discretion" in which this ethnographic research took place. After illustrating the methodological choices and describing the first day in the observed local office, labour inspectors' discretionary practices are described, starting with the room in which the bureaucratic meeting with the worker takes place and in which inspectors make decisions on the management of work irregularities.

The rooms observed are the complaint desk, the dispute-settlement procedures room, and the labour inspectors' office in which the back-office work takes place. The field observations led to the following preliminary considerations: (1) pressures in policy directions related to workplace irregularity controls have increased the standardisation of procedures; (2) pressures are aimed at accountability, resulting in inspectors being pushed to solve the most cases with minimal waste of resources; (3) public pressures are classified as priorities for action or perceptions of the severity of cases, leading to some areas being neglected and some types of workers being given less attention; and (4) certain characteristics of street-level bureaucrats, such as their gender, years of experience, and type of studies conducted, create differences in the way work irregularities are handled.

Keywords Ethnography • Field note • Discretion • Labour inspectors • Bureaucratic encounter

R. Paraciani, *Labour Inspectors in Italy*,
https://doi.org/10.1007/978-3-031-37997-0_4

4.1 Observing Labour Inspectors

To understand how labour inspectors resolve ambiguities of different orders and types in cases legally defined as labour exploitation, I observed their daily activities to see them in action. After several months of negotiating my position, I faced my "first day of school," aware of the need to consider and reconsider my position and role within the inspectorate (Semi, 2010). My presence was comparable to that of an intern, and I was interested in the management of labour irregularities, particularly those that were included in the legal definition of "labour exploitation." I conducted a discovery observation. All the inspectors and surveyors were aware of my identity as a doctoral student in sociology and my interest in labour irregularities, which is why I earned the nickname "the Trainee of Hardship" (field note). Although my role and the reason for my presence were known, not all the inspectors understood that they were the object of the research. I joined labour inspectors in three stages that corresponded to three decision-making moments in the process of resolving labour irregularity cases. The three rooms of discretion in which labour inspectors were observed are as follows: (1) the complaints desk, (2) the dispute-settlement procedure room, and (3) the labour inspectors' offices in which the back-office work occurred. For security reasons, it was not possible for me to take part in workplace inspections, so I was only able to deal with cases in the back-office stage.

Participating in labour inspectors' work takes time. Observing the ways in which inspectors handled different labour irregularities from their perspective allowed me to determine their decision-making methods and understand the motivations behind their choices. Their speech was also a very important aspect, including not only conversations with users but also informal exchanges characterised by decisiveness, immediacy, and spontaneity. These moments allowed me to look beyond the facts, understand beliefs and feelings, and determine the criteria for action and pressures, thereby highlighting the relational dynamics within the field.

As reiterated in many methodological texts (e.g., Marradi, 2007; Silverman & Marvasti, 2008; Maxwell, 2013; Bryman, 2016), the observer modifies the observed situation just by being there. This is why the way in which the field presents itself to the researcher is relevant, which is how the labour inspectors presented themselves to a young researcher in this case. For example, I was invited to join the labour inspectors for their coffee break several times, and several inspectors asked me to bring them coffee.

During the long period of observation, my role inevitably changed. From being "one of the new trainees," I became "the trainee," to then being "the doctoral student," and finally "Rebecca" (field note). These different roles entail different responsibilities within the ethnographic field. For example, as a learner, I was given a different role: "She is the one who studies us." I requested the labour inspectors' suggestions and opinions and also asked them to share their work-related frustrations and dissatisfactions. My presence was accepted and, over time, understood. However, it was also negotiated in terms of my entry into the field as well as what I could do and my ability to "go … with the flow" (Cardano, 2011, p. 110, my translation), which included what I found myself doing (e.g., making photocopies, handling Excel files, bringing in documents, and running errands). My playing these different roles allowed me to observe different rooms from different perspectives.

4.2 The Local Office

> Today is my first day in the inspectorate, and I am lost. I am supposed to get to Savio's ([a] labour inspector's) office, but I … realise that it is on the second floor. Upon arriving at the floor, no one opens the door for me; however, I manage to get in [due to] an inspector who stamps my badge. There is a machine to punch in and out as soon as you walk through the glass door. Although at first no one seemed to notice my entry on the second floor, I am stopped by an inspector on my fourth pass in front of her door. She comes out unnerved and in a scolding voice asks me what I am doing there, telling me that that is the second, not the first, floor and that only the first floor is open to the public. I explain that I am a doctoral student and that I have an appointment with Savio. She immediately changes her expression, smiles at me, and walks me to the right door. To get there, we turn … right, right again, and finally left. (Field note, January 2017)

The office within which the observations were conducted is one of 80 territorial offices throughout the country. The director of the office is responsible for allocating resources and for managing the supervision, conciliation, and training of the inspectors in his office.

> Of course we have national guidelines, but they are not enough. We still have to be able to [build] everything to make these national formulas consistent and homogeneous with the style of our organisation. [There are many] threads to unravel to … [ensure] homogeneity in the office and to

figure out who to delegate to [and] with whom to share my responsibilities. (Field note, June 2017, The director)

The observed office was divided into six macro areas (Fig. 4.5). Of these six, there were four areas of activity involving labour inspectors: the regional liaison unit; supervision processes; planning, control, and operation processes; and user services processes. The additional activities were carried out by carabiniers or administrative staff. An inspector could have been part of more than one macro area as they could have either been a member of an inspection team or the regional liaison unit. Alternatively, they could have either been on duty at the counter or involved in the process of planning, controlling, and operating the office's activities.

There were 45 labour inspectors in the entire office, and the rest of the staff were administrative. The latter were dedicated to activities that require fast processing, "to the papers" (field note), while the labour inspectors were those front-line professionals who handled the entire chain of the request for action (i.e., from the complaint by the worker to the eventual inspection and sanction) and monitored the territory spontaneously based on anonymous reports and situations considered particularly at risk of irregularity. Junior inspectors were enlisted through the second to last public competition to become a labour inspector that occurred in 2004,[1] and senior inspectors were divided between those who entered the service through competitions prior to the 2004 competition and those who entered without a competition and through career advancement. The main difference between those who entered the profession through open competition or not lies in the potential inspector having a degree. Before the competition, an upper secondary school degree was sufficient, but inspectors later required degrees in law, political science, or economics.

The main activities observed during the ethnographic activity were divided into two processes: the supervisory process (i.e., one-on-one conciliation, inspection activities, and back-office work) and the user service process (i.e., requests for action). The office is part of a multi-story building that houses other organisations, such as insurance companies, law firms, and commercial firms. The first to third floors belong to the National

[1] The last public competition to become labor inspectors was in 2022, 18 years after the previous one. The research was conducted between 2017 and 2019; therefore, information on new hires remains out.

Labour Inspectorate, all of which are organised in the same way, with the only difference being that there is a meeting hall also used for conducting training courses and a complaints desk on the first floor. Each floor is circular with a central inner courtyard. The stairs for walking access revolve around the two elevators on the ground floor. The floor plans of the observed office's three floors can be seen in Fig. 4.1.

The first floor is the only one open to the public: on Mondays through Fridays from 09:15 am to 12:00 pm as well as from 15:00 pm to 17:00 pm on Mondays and Thursdays. The office and first floor are closed on Saturdays and Sundays. Four identical A4 sheets indicate this to the public (Fig. 4.2): one on the stairs, one outside the elevator, one next to it, and one on the glass door of the second floor. The sheets, posted by labour inspectors, include a black-and-white index finger that indicates the direction in which the office can be found.

> It happens often [that we] find people everywhere. 'I have to report,' they tell you. Then we have to send them to the first floor. They go to the first floor, [and] they [can't] find their way. They go up and come back to us: 'What room on the second floor?' And then, it may sound absurd to you, but sometimes the easiest thing to do is to take one floor of stairs down, one floor up, and accompany them in person. (Field note, March 2017, Marika, a labour inspector)

> Rosanna tells me, laughing, that the other day, during a one-man conciliation, they interrupted her three times. And all three times were people who were lost. "I attached the signs one by one because I couldn't take it anymore! And, yet, I get interrupted while trying to talk to some workers. How do we look?" Field note, March 2017

The first difficulty for the user is identifying the correct floor. Except for the signs shown in Fig. 4.2, there are no other indications that only the first floor is open to the public. On the doorbell outside the building, in the elevator, and on floors 1, 2, and 3, there is only a generic sign saying "National Labour Inspectorate." In order to prevent users from entering the wrong floor, a sign was posted on the doors of the second and third floors that read "DISMISSALS, COMPLAINTS, INFORMATION: FIRST FLOOR. You are on the second/third floor!" (Fig. 4.3).

Once workers get past this obstacle and find the correct floor, there is no reception desk or information point, but there is a small entrance from which a corridor runs from the left and right. Several A4 sheets of paper

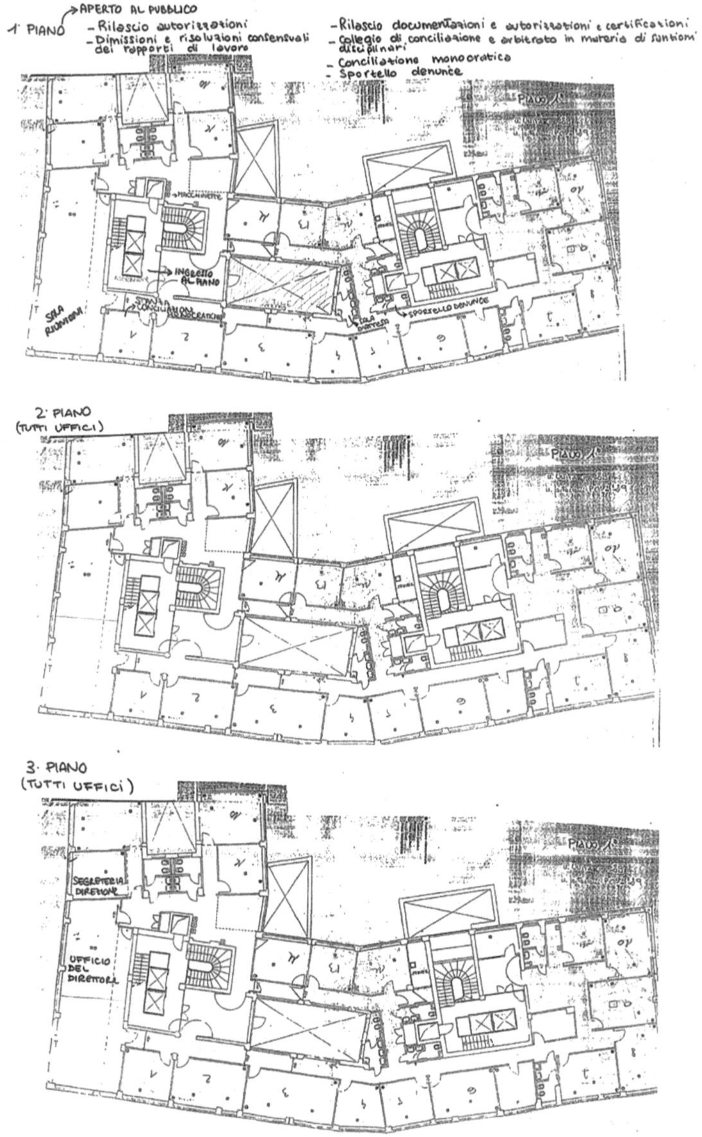

Fig. 4.1 The floor plans of the observed territorial site's three floors. (Source: Field notes)

Fig. 4.2 Photograph of the sign. (Source: Field notes)

are hanging on the wall that state "COMPLAINTS OFFICE," which indicates the way for those interested in filing a complaint. The difficulties encountered in accessing the National Labour Inspectorate's public offices causes complications in the inspectors' work as they are often interrupted by users who have lost their way. It also disturbs the user's calmness as, in many cases, the user arrives at the meeting not well disposed since the first contact with the service takes a form similar to that of a refusal. Physical barriers, in fact, reflect and reproduce the boundaries that organisations create between the "inside" and "outside."

> Today I spent two hours in the entrance room on the first floor. I set about collecting field notes sitting at the table in front of the entrance door. A total of 14 people arrived. Some had to file a complaint, some had to sign resignations, and some had an appointment for one-on-one conciliations. All of them, after looking around, turned to me for information. One labour con-

Fig. 4.3 The sign attached to the third-floor door. (Translation: RESIGNATION COMPLAINTS INFORMATION FIRST floor. Source: Field notes)

sultant ... [from] the inspectorate [who asked me] to stand in for her client during a conciliation, tells me, huffing, that you never know where you have to go. (Field note, April 2017)

Gregorio is more nervous than usual today. I ask him during a coffee break if everything is okay. He laughs, asking me if I am teasing him because he thought I knew the joke. I was not aware of it. The day before yesterday, someone from outside the Inspectorate came to the third floor and entered his office (the one closest to the entrance to the floor) ... and stole his bag with his wallet, various documents, and service PC inside. "Rebecca, Rebecca. Does all this coming and going seem possible to you? Does it seem possible to you that I was robbed leaving things in my office where I work every day? To me, frankly, it sounds like a joke! That said: never leave anything in the offices. Let [this] at least serve as a lesson to us." (Field note, April 2017, Gregorio, a labour inspector)

4.3 The Complaints Desk

The complaints desk room is where workers go to file their request for action by reporting one or more irregularities concerning their current or previous employment (Fig. 4.4). The possibility of laying a complaint via e-mail without going to the counter had recently been introduced, but this practice as still uncommon. In fact, the inspectors on duty did not regard it as a practice. Moreover, if a worker telephoned, they were told to come to the Inspectorate in person and file a complaint.

Augustine tells me that … when he answers the phone and … the caller starts to complain about their condition, he can tell them to send the request for action through the Internet. "But, look, I realised that it was more complicated for me to … explain … it than to have him come in person to make the complaint, so now I don't even say it anymore." Field note, June 2017

The door separating the complaints desk from the small waiting room comprised only a doorframe without a door (Fig. 4.4).

To get to the complaints counter there is a long waiting line, preceding the "door without a door" (that's what they call it). People wait while standing. Today, I counted 14, but there are … five uncomfortable, wooden chairs attached to the wall. Between the five chairs and the door without a door, [there is] a strip outlined with black scotch tape, and, on the wall, a sheet printed from Word in bold caps stating "**CONTINUES WAIT HERE.**"

There are two inspectors on duty, and they work simultaneously every morning from 09:00 am to 12:00 pm and two afternoons a week from 15:00 pm to 17:00 pm. They sit next to each other and are separated from the workers by a desk. There is no plexiglass window, which is unusual in public bureaucracies.

I ask Gregory why they made this choice. He laughs and tells me that the choice is not a choice. "It just happened, we are renting here, and this was the room on the first floor that was smaller than the one we used as a meeting room but big enough to take complaints and with enough chairs for people to sit." He also says that plexiglass would not be bad because, in the end, it is a form of protection and, in these cases, you never know. Each

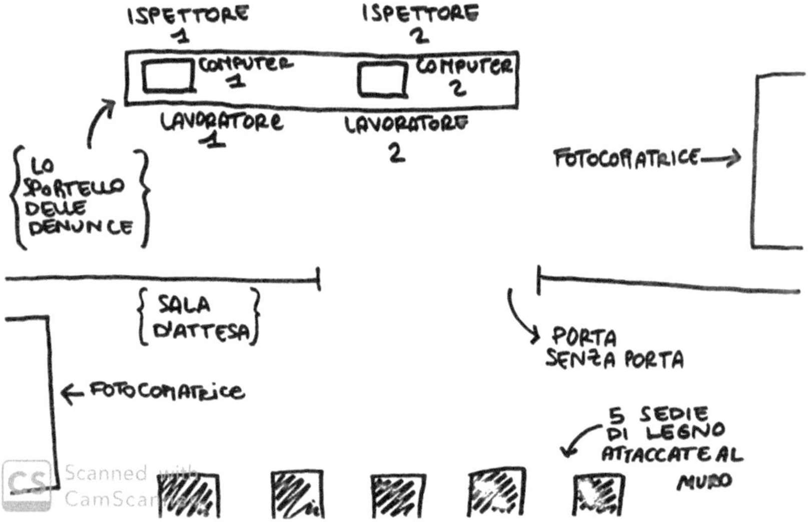

Fig. 4.4 The complaints desk. (Translation from left to the right: Copy machine, (Waiting room), (The complaints desk), Inspector 1; Computer 1; Worker 1; Inspector 2; Computer 2; Worker 2; Copy machine; Door without a door; Five wooden chairs attached to the wall; Source: Field notes)

> inspector has a computer in front of him on which they formalise the request for action.
>
> To the right of the counter is a photocopier (there is also one in the waiting room), which leads to administrators and inspectors, who are grappling with the paperwork of bureaucracy, coming and going. Everything contributes to making this room extremely chaotic. The absence of a door makes the buzz constant, even during the formalisation of the call to action. (Field note, February 2017)

This is the first physical place within which the bureaucratic encounter takes place (Hasenfeld et al., 1987), which occurs through the interaction between different but inseparable roles and powers: that of the small bureaucrat and that of the worker (Dubois, 2010). The former needs the cooperation of the worker in order to succeed despite adverse working conditions, including high workloads, scarce resources, and limited time, and the latter depends on the street-level bureaucrat to provide them with the benefits and services managed by them (Tummers et al., 2015). Although they need each other, the relationship remains asymmetrical (Mik-Meyer & Silverman, 2019). Indeed, labour inspectors are in a position of power over service users because theirs is a power role (Merton, 1940; Zacka, 2017) as they control users' behaviour through the discretionary power they have (Hupe, 2013). Similarly, citizens' dependence on the services provided can turn into deference as the waiting time (i.e., before being received and in the entire handling of the case), the lack of knowledge of the functioning of the "steel cage" (Weber, 1997), and the fact that labour inspectors have the last word emphasise the asymmetry of the administrative relationship. The spatial arrangement of the complaints desk reflected this hierarchy. It was the desk that, despite separating labour inspectors from workers by a few steps, signalled a separation between these two figures who had different roles, identities, and powers. The physical artefacts reflected symbolic aspects, thereby filling this encounter with meaning. The worker, in most cases, arrived at the desk after getting lost and having waited their turn for at least a couple of hours while standing or, if they are lucky, sitting on one of the wooden chairs attached to the wall. When the worker managed to pass through the door without a door and reach the counter, the confusion as such that the interaction often took place at a very high volume. This noise pollution was caused by three main factors: (a) the absence of a door between the counter and the waiting room; (b) the presence of two photocopiers in the space, which was an indispensable object; and (c) two workers simultaneously laying their complaints at the same counter with two different inspectors.

These two inspectors do not perform this activity exclusively. Until four years ago, the labour inspectors covered the shift at the counter one day per month on a rotating basis. Subsequently, a smaller group of labour inspectors was created who cover this shift on rotation as well. There were five inspectors at the complaints desk in the observed location: three male and two female. Only one of these devoted most of their time to this activity, while two were also part of the inspections programme and two took part in the one-on-one conciliations. In the case of need, this role was filled by other inspectors. This shortlist of inspectors was created for this activity because not all of them gave the same importance to the request for the action.

> Inspector Fausto tells me that … the time he spent at the complaints desk seemed like lost work time. He did not feel useful. He prefers to go into the

field [as] he feels [like] "an operative, not a bureaucrat." (Field note, December 2017)

If this task is viewed as a waste of time, it is likely to result in poor service, according to the director.

The director, in explaining to me how he makes decisions about the various roles, says that he has gotten to know the people he works with and that everyone has their own aptitude[s]: Some are better with numbers, some are better with logic, some have intuition, and some have a way with people. (Field note, April 2017)

In this space, therefore, the inspector on duty at the counter was considered suitable (either by personal characteristics or attitudinal characteristics) for this role.

Most users waited while standing, and the inspector at the counter called workers one by one. There was no automatic calling device, and the wait was about one-hour long. Isolation between the waiting space and the counter space was virtually non-existent due to the door without a door, which simultaneously allowed the waiting room to be kept under control from inside the room by assessing the turnout. The long queue affected the quality of the relationship. Time is one of those resources that street-level bureaucrats had to account for on a daily basis as the counter was timetabled. A large turnout risked hasty interactions between inspectors and workers, which could have resulted in an incomplete complaint that had insufficient information for beginning an investigation, leading to a lack of information needed for making a decision.

Today, the line at the complaint counter is particularly long. The air is heavy and the noise pollution particularly annoying. One of the two inspectors on duty, Simona, looks at me, putting her hands in her hair, and says, "Today you have to run, run, run." She gets up from her desk and, arriving at the door without a door, shouts, "Next!" (Field note, March 2017)

Inspectors getting up to call users positively affected the relationship as the worker was made to feel welcomed for the first time since entering the service. The door without a door demarcated the transition between being onstage and offstage, or, following Goffman, marked the transition from one scene to another for users. In the waiting room, most of the time, the worker was unnerved by the effort made to find the right place, the waiting time, and the fact that, in all likelihood, they had to stand while waiting. Having crossed the threshold, the meeting materialised and, with it, the different roles were enacted: having crossed the door without a door, the user was polite and docile and tried to speak calmly with a low tone of voice. This was also to avoid being overheard by the worker next door, who was laying a complaint with the second inspector on duty at the counter. However, the tone rose and the mask collapsed in cases where the worker felt misunderstood or unheard.

> The worker is struggling to understand the labour inspector's demands. She did not bring the necessary documentation to file the complaint. She will probably have to return to complete her ... request for action. However, she is not understanding the reasons. She starts screaming that bureaucracy does not work and that trying to obtain a right is merely a waste of time. The inspector at the counter urges her to calm down and remains seated at her computer. The worker leaves, cursing. The inspector, turning to me, tells me that it takes patience, a lot of patience, to do this job. (Field note, April 2017)

Once meeting each other, the bureaucratic meeting takes place (Zacka, 2017). At the complaints desk, this moment consisted of three main stages: (a) checking the worker's identity; (b) gathering information; and (c) deciding how to process the case. The first stage is used by Dubois (2010) as an example of the possible exercise of symbolic violence, which is a type of violence that is difficult to perceive and asks individuals to define their identity.

> Domestic worker: "I am a domestic worker, assisting an elderly person at home."
>
> Labour inspector Augustine: "Okay, so she is a caregiver." (Field note, May 2017)

> The Moroccan national worker is keeping his gaze down while the labour inspector continues to ask pressing questions: What is the type of contract he had? What kind of housing is he staying in? Is he unemployed now? Is he doing odd jobs? ... As we are having coffee, the inspector tells me that, by now, she has realised that there are different categories of workers who come to the complaint counter:

- Those who have been paid off the books and want to be paid again;
- Those who merely want to get back at their employer by procuring an inspection "just in case" and who exaggerate their own situation; and
- Those who are really in need and come to report something very small.

> The right technique is to play good cop and bad cop, by asking them many questions and making them feel [as though they are] under scrutiny. (Field note, August 2017)

In most of the cases observed, however, it was often the workers who arrived with folders full of documentation and who reported each piece of information as accurately as possible, making the filing of the complaint quicker. Additionally, there were only three occurrences of foreign workers not being in possession of their residence documents. This indicates that, either due to the fear of having to leave the country or due to a lack of knowledge on the labour regulations for irregular foreigners, spontaneous reporting of one's status is a very delicate and, above all, rare step (FRA, 2015).

At the complaints desk, the labour inspectors decided how to record the request for action, with two trends being noted. Some inspectors preferred to transcribe the request for action word-for-word, almost as if the worker wrote it themselves. Indeed, in some of these cases, a statement written and signed by the worker was attached to the file. These inspectors asked the worker a variety of questions related to co-workers, the presence of any witnesses (whose names, surnames, and telephone numbers were also requested), and the employers' habits.

> Today, during the recording of a call to action, the worker was asked to handwrite a list of people who could corroborate her testimony. When I asked why the statement was … handwritten, I was told that the more details there are, the less effort will be made in the investigation. Because "there is no hard case or easy case, only [a] good or bad call to action." (Field note, March 2017)

> I ask Marika why she prefer[s] to extend the time it [takes] to collect the complaint by asking the workers many questions. She replie[s] that, in this way, regardless of whether the inspection is feasible or not, the worker leaves with a positive feeling because he or she [feels] heard. (Field note, April 2017)

This view is not shared by all inspectors as the second trend entailed recording the worker's complaint in a schematic manner. The reasons behind this related mainly to the number of complaints that can be recorded by shortening the waiting time.

> Augustine tells me he disagrees with his colleagues at the counter who ask workers too many questions. "The reason why I think it is better to collect as many requests for action as possible is that, this way, we have more material and more cases. And … ask[ing] for the names of key witnesses or other details is pointless as there will be a way in the right forum to do a full preliminary interview with the worker. That is why I think it is only a waste of time."(Field note, April 2017)

Labour inspectors also used their discretion to decide whether to offer the worker the administrative solution of a dispute-settlement procedure or to proceed directly to the inspection, thereby initiating the actual investigation. The observed territorial office was characterised by its resolution of many cases through the conciliatory solution. This is because, at the organisational level, it was informally decided to offer all complainants this solution to first speed up the time taken for each case since it takes much less time to find an economic agreement between the parties rather than initiating investigative proceedings and because the justice system's time is considered to be excessively slow. Therefore, the conciliatory solution provided workers with a better chance of obtaining money in a shorter period of time when redressing wage and contribution irregularities. Despite the guidelines and standards established by the Inspectorate, which states that the labour inspectors should propose settling the dispute in conciliation when filing complaints, not all inspectors at the counter proposed the conciliatory solution to all workers when filing a complaint. Different trends were noted in the cases observed. To the workers who reported one or more irregularities within the domestic work sector, the conciliatory solution was not only proposed but strongly recommended.

> Fausto explains to me that, in the case of domestic work, if there are no immigration problems and no obvious criminal violations, conciliation with the family is attempted in 100 percent of cases. The parties are called and an agreement is reached whereby the family pays the worker what they had to pay, regulari[sing] the labour relationship on the contribution side, and the inspection stops avoiding penalties. … The agreement [needs to] regularise the situation [through] either … report[ing] in full or [making] variations

that are justified. "I went back to my country and was there three months" can be a justification. (Field note, April 2017)

But not all people who reported irregularities similar to those typically present in the domestic work sector were offered the conciliatory solution, especially if the worker was employed in the logistics sector.

A worker has just … reported a situation very similar to the previous one (the previous one involved a domestic worker of Filipino origin). The worker has not been offered a conciliatory solution. The inspector closes the file, on top of which he places a post-it note that reads "LOGISTICS." I ask Augustine why he did not propose the solution of one-on-one conciliation to the worker in question. He tells me that "logistics is [in] the eye of the storm" and that, as an inspectorate, we need to give these situations the highest priority; we need to do inspections, not conciliations. (Field note, March 2017)

Furthermore, the majority of workers who accepted the conciliatory solution were foreigners.

Marika tells me that with them (meaning foreigners), it is easier to make them accept conciliatory solutions. Just say that "It's a way to get the money sooner." Of course, she is talking about foreigners with regular residence permits. (Field note, March 2017)

According to Gregorio, Italians tend not to accept the conciliatory solution when filing a complaint because "They are more angry and less desperate." (Field note, May 2017)

Augustine propose[s] to the worker of Italian descent employed in the construction industry the solution of a dispute-settlement procedure, explaining it in detail. The worker laughs and says he does not understand the point. He stresses the absence of penalties for the employer … and says he "wants to make the employer pay for it all." (Field note, March 2017)

Labour inspectors with more experience tended to propose dispute-settlement procedures in most cases, in line with organisational arrangements, but they emphasised the negative aspects of this avenue and criticised it in informal interactions with workers.

Serena … explain[s] the possibilities and limitations of the conciliatory solution to the worker employed as a waiter in the restaurant industry. [She] emphasises the fact that the employer will go unpunished and that, by settling the dispute here, [the worker] will get the money first but less than he would be entitled to and that, above all, would be a somewhat unfair result. "Decide for yourself whether you would rather have some money in three months or whether you think you should get something more in terms of justice." (Field note, April 2017)

I see Arianna [is] contrite. She tells me that sometimes she gets nervous doing this work and doesn't always understand the point of conciliation. "From 1996 to 2004, we were doing eight inspections a day, everything was simple, procedures were streamlined, and there were fewer bureaucratic quibbles. Today, everything is cumbersome, and sometimes it seems like a waste of time. We are more interested in making numbers than doing well." (Field note, September 2017)

4.4 The Dispute-Settlement Procedure Room

The dispute-settlement procedure room is where workers, after agreeing to settle the dispute with this … solution, try to reach an economic agreement with the employer. Here, the inspector is a third and impartial actor, a kind of mediator, whose task is to restore the labour relationship that is irregular in terms of wages and … contributions. By settling the dispute here, the employer is exempt from any kind of penalty. The room is small and bare. The labour inspector sits facing the door, behind an old computer monitor that covers his face. The worker and employer sit on the other side of the desk, next to each other. The window is large but covered by a sheet of white paper that filters the light. On it is written "The window is broken, please keep it closed." I sit next to the inspector; I am not covered by the computer. (Field note, March 2017)

The institution of dispute-settlement procedures was introduced by Legal Decree 124/2004. It is an instrument of a non-repressive nature that is to be offered, according to the law, as an alternative function to the traditional inspections by supervisory bodies. With the latest reform of the National Labour Inspectorate, established by Legal Decree 149/2015 for the rationalisation and simplification of inspection activities in the field of labour and social legislation, the preventive conciliatory tool (proposed to the worker at the time of request for intervention), the use of which is applied at the discretion of the individual administration by law, has become the preferred solution. The reasons, as already seen, mainly concern the expansion of the INL's scope of intervention (and thus the consequent increase in the workload) and the possibility of speeding up and completing the greater number of requests for intervention. Regulatory provisions prohibit the possibility of finding an economic agreement in compensatory terms in this case.

The dispute-settlement procedure room is located on the second floor, which is the floor open to the public. This, unlike the complaints desk, does not have a waiting room outside it but, instead, has a door. In the observed territorial office, each conciliation lasted one hour: the first dispute was from 09:00 am to 10:00 am and the last was from 12:00 pm to 13:00 pm, for a total of four conciliations per day, Monday through Friday. The meetings took place by appointment. When it was time for conciliation, the inspector on duty opened the door and invited the employee and employer into the room, who then sat on the same side of the desk, emphasising the equality of the relationship. By settling the dispute here, the employer is exempt from any kind of penalty, provided that the wage or contribution irregularity is remedied. During conciliation, both parties may be represented by attorneys or, in the case of companies, labour consultants or, in the case of workers, union representatives. Except in rare cases in which the parties arrive at the meeting with an already established agreement, it is very difficult to resolve the situation in one meeting; two to four meetings are required for successful one-on-one conciliation. Approximately three months elapse between meetings. This implies that the inspector moderating the conciliation does not always follow the previous steps and that they do not always remember the specifics of the individual situation.

> Augustine does not remember what was established in the previous session. The worker and the labour consultant are arguing two different things, starting to raise their voices, which is why Augustine decides to intervene: "I would remind you that you have one hour … and that there is only half an hour left. I … need to know what we had said in the previous [sessions]." (Field note, February 2017)

In cases where conciliation is unsuccessful, which can happen due to either one of the parties' unwillingness or the inspector assessing the situation as irreconcilable, the traditional investigation and inspection process begins. This is not the venue, therefore, for testimony and evidence: It is the room where the request for intervention starts and where "the most mutually beneficial solution for both parties" (field note) is identified.

Each morning, there was only one inspector-conciliator. As with the complaints desk, for the dispute-settlement procedure room, the director of the territorial office decided not to have the inspectors perform only this activity. Thus, a shortlist of inspectors was created who carried out this phase, and they covered this shift on a rotating basis. There were four inspectors: three female and one male, with one of the female inspectors covering two days, not just one as the others did. In case of absences or periods of leave or illness, there were three male substitutes. Thus, people deemed suitable for conciliation or who indicated a willingness to take part in this phase also acted in this space.

Except for a few extraordinary cases, the one-hour time limit was adhered to by all but one of the inspectors, who prolonged the duration of conciliations, which had a negative effect on subsequent conciliations because, unlike complaints, for which waiting is an integral part of the request for action, conciliation is by appointment.

Generally, conciliation began with the labour inspector getting up, opening the door, and seating both parties (and possibly their legal representatives) inside the room. After this was the identification phase, which took longer at the first conciliatory meetings as at least two people were present. After that, the conciliatory attempt began.

> Inspector Arianna is leafing through the file of the next case to be reconciled, … [with the relevant people] waiting behind the closed door. It is [the] first meeting in [the] conciliation. "There will be laughter again today," she tells me, shaking her head. Then she gets up, goes the long way around the desk, and … opens the door. "Next!" … A restaurant worker of Pakistani origin accompanied by a union representative and the employer represented by a business consultant enter. Once seated, the ritual begins. Arianna reads the call to action aloud as she begins to … fill out the minutes, her head behind the large computer screen. Only after entering the information of the case in question into the present Word [document] does she move the screen and address the parties. "We don't have time to waste here. The purpose of conciliation is not to get evidence or to shut down the company. We are here, as adults, just to make it all add up and, based on what was stated in the complaint, come up with a figure that makes sense. If we don't finish today, we make another appointment. This solution suits everyone: She (points to the worker) has a chance to see some money within a short time. You (… addresses the employer) avoid an inspection. And with inspections, we always find something wrong." After this introduction, the identification phase begins: Each person in the room must be identified. At

> least one photocopy must be made for each document, including residence permits [for foreign workers]. (Field note, February 2017)

> The domestic worker is crying. She is a caregiver of Moldavian origin who has been working for over two years … with the Green family to care for Mr Green's father. She is accusing Mr Green, sitting next to her, of treating her like a slave. She says that, in addition to not receiving wages in her last period of work, she was forced to sleep in a very small room without even a bed and had no days off. Mr Verdi calls her a liar. In all this, Inspector Sandro is silent; he is not intervening. At the word "liar," the worker pulls out her phone and shows us pictures of a very small and bare room, with an open cot leaning against the wall and two photographs taped to the walls. Sandro interjects, saying, "This is not the place to show evidence. One must come here to conciliate, not to prove who knows what." (Field note, April 2017)

One of the special features of this institution concerns the type of interaction that characterises the bureaucratic encounter. It is not a classic user-small bureaucrat interaction but a three-way interaction: worker, bureaucrat, and employer, in which the labour inspector has a superior position over the other two parties. This is represented in the spatial organisation of the interview, with the labour inspector on one side of the desk and the worker and employer on the other side, next to each other (Fig. 4.5). Additionally, in this room, the worker and employer are in the same position in line with reconciliation guidelines, which specify that the employer and worker should be heard simultaneously, in the same room, thereby giving both an opportunity to hear each other's statements (Leonardi et al., 2021). However, situations were also observed in which the inspector found it necessary to hear the worker separately by having the employer leave the room:

> The worker, a saleswoman of Romanian origin, complaining of not receiving a salary and working under conditions of great control and blackmail, is screaming at her employer, almost crying as he laughs at her, calling her crazy, seeking complicity from me and the inspector. Rosanna at this point decides to make the employer leave and let the worker calm down and then asks her questions about her situation with the door closed, without the antagonistic party in the room. … I ask Rosanna why she decided to separate the parties. She tells me that she understood that the worker was inhibited by the presence of her former boss and that if she did not do so, they

Fig. 4.5 The dispute-settlement procedure room. (Translation from left to the right: Window covered with paper; Inspector; Computer; Desk; Worker; Employer; Brings. Source: Field notes)

would not be able to come to an agreement and, therefore, the conciliation would fail. (Field note, June 2017)

This also brings into question the alleged equality of the employer's and employee's positions. The latter, despite sitting on the same side of the desk as their (in most cases former) employer, often were at a disadvantage compared to the employer in this room. Most of the workers who accepted the conciliatory proposal at the application stage were foreigners. Among the possible interpretations, it is possible to assume that Italian workers have a network that allows them to wait the necessary time to obtain justice by "doing everything to get the company the [consequences] it deserves" (field note). On the other hand, one of the reasons may lie in the fact that, in some cases, the lack of language competency during the first meeting at the complaints desk makes it complicated for labour inspectors to explain fully what one-on-one conciliation is, merely emphasising the fact that it is "easier to get something done as soon as possible" (field note). This implies that most workers in these conciliations are foreigners who have a poor command of Italian.

> The domestic worker is of Filipino origin. She is not assisted by a legal representative but by [who] we … understand to be her sister. The sister's role is to act as interpreter because the worker does not speak a word of Italian or even understand it. The problem is that the sister also does not have a great command of Italian, which makes communication very difficult. Inspector Rosanna, in order to make herself understood, begins to raise her tone of voice and stand up at her desk. The employer shakes his head, unnerved, and says, "This is crazy stuff. What could she have reported [when] she can't even speak Italian?" (Field note, March 2017)

> Inspector Renata proceeds in order. After bringing in and seating the parties, she explains the institution of one-on-one conciliation. She begins to speak citing the relevant legislation using technical and legal language. The domestic worker, of Ukrainian origin, shakes her head. "I don't understand. If you talk like that, I don't understand you. She talks too difficult for me!" Jenna responds, saying that this is the law and the law speaks clearly. If she cannot understand the law, "It will be difficult to find a solution, so [you] better make an effort to listen." (Field note, February 2017)

In most of the conciliations observed, the employers expressed closeness to the inspector. In fact, several interactions were recorded during conciliation that demonstrated employers approaching inspectors with the belief that they share the same social affiliation (Cottino, 2005) and problems, seeking understanding and using moral disengagement techniques (Zamperini, 1998) such as euphemistic labelling to downplay the effects of their actions.

> The employer speaks by addressing only Inspector Sandro. He admits that he has had some problems with the … last two monthly payments, and once the economic agreement has been reached and the payment arrangements established, he turns to Sandro: "You know even better than I how these things work. We have so many things to think about that sometimes we commit minor infractions." (Field note, September 2017)

In this room, the labour inspector can decide on the ways in which to handle this difficult three-way interaction, whether by using highly technical language, creating distance between those who understand it and those who do not; by separating the parties, creating a space that gives the worker a greater openness to dialogue; or by strictly adhering to the time limits imposed by the conciliation procedure. Differences emerged in how similar labour irregularities were handled according to different productive sectors. Although most of the settlement attempts concerned labour irregularities in domestic work, there was no shortage of cases involving the logistics sector, which were considered the most serious “and in the eye of the media storm” (field note). In cases related to domestic work, even when there were clear indications of severe exploitation and blatant irregularities, such as sleeping in a cot in a small room with no windows, being subjected to the control of food and phone calls, or even physical violence (as in one case in conciliation), it is argued that “this is not the place to gather evidence, because it suits [them] to try to conciliate in order to get some money in a short time” (field note). In the cases concerning the logistics sector, however, the opposite trend was recorded. Indeed, in most of these situations, not only did the inspector tend to have a harsher tone with the employer, but they also refused conciliation and proceeded directly to the inspection stage. Cases involving workers in the logistics sector also almost always occurred at the open door. This was because these were often controversial circumstances and there was the fear that, especially on the part of the company, it could result in situations that were dangerous to the inspector’s safety. A simple request such as “Can you open the door so that we can circulate the air a little?” allowed inspectors to control possible changes in tone and, if necessary, to intervene from the outside.

The differences between labour inspectors with more experience were also evident at this stage. Those with less experience tended to use highly technical and legal language, to be less “empathetic” towards the workers, and to implement behaviours typical of Merton’s (1940) ritualist conciliator, who embraces institutionalised norms and enacts routinised behaviours. The ritualist conciliator intervenes in discussions for the sole purpose of requesting data and information to be included in the minutes of the session, to remind the parties that the time is running out and that an agreement must be reached, to schedule another appointment, and to verify the correctness of the figures proposed by the parties. Inspectors with more years of experience, on the other hand, tended to implement personalisation strategies (Brodkin, 2008; Dubois, 2010). Indeed, some inspectors used the technique of bluffing with the employer, pretending to have information they did not actually have or making the employer believe that if they did not cooperate, an inspection would be conducted shortly. In most cases, it was not the same inspector who followed all stages of the one-on-one conciliation. However, in some cases, the waiting time was extended in order to allow inspectors to personally handle the conciliation from the first to the last meeting.

> Inspector Rosanna typically takes more than three months between meetings to be the inspector on duty and handle the conciliation from start to finish. I ask … her why she made this decision and she tells me that, after so many years … she realised that it is not an extra month that compromises her work: "I prefer to be slower but do things with my own. It's a personal sense. I have my own style." (Field note, March 2017)

4.5 Inspectors' Offices and Back-Office Work

Labour inspectors' offices were where most of the back-office work took place. In these offices, each inspector had their own space to prepare the information needed to collect evidence necessary for the inspection. The inspection preparation phase is a preparatory activity and establishes the type of information and documentation to be collected and how to proceed. In these same offices, minutes were prepared, and documents and statements acquired during the inspection phase were sorted. According to the code of conduct for labour inspectors, case information should not be shared. For this reason, there were two large cabinets in each room, one for each inspector, and each equipped with a key. Desk drawers could also be locked to protect sensitive data.

> Inspector Savio receives me in his office. It is a yellow and brown space. There are two desks: Savio's and that of an inspector who is temporarily out of the office for an inspection. As he explains to me how the office activities are organised and what my duties will be for the coming months, he points out his colleague's desk: an empty brown desk, with only a PC riser, a desk phone, and a desk calendar. "She is rigorous," he specifies. He also tells me that, according to the regulations, all inspectors' desks should be like this. And then he adds, pointing out to me the mass of papers and files on top of [his desk], that "They are all unnecessary formalities. Just spending ten minutes in the hallway is enough to know everything about everyone." (Field note, January 2017)

Space management in line with the regulations was seen in only 6 offices out of the 17 observed. This space, unlike that open to the public, was an environment that labour inspectors tended to personalise with plants, children's drawings, pictures, and photographs on the walls.

I notice that Sarah has hanging on the wall a nursery rhyme by Gianni Rodari entitled *The Colors of Crafts*:

> I know the smells of the trades:
> Of nutmeg know the grocers,
> Tastes like oil on the worker's overalls,
> Of flour knows the baker,
> They know about land the peasants,
> Of paint the painters,
> On the doctor's white coat
> Of medicine smells good.
> Slackers, strange though,
> They don't taste like anything, and they smell a little bit.

> The office is very hot [as it is] exposed to the sun, and we are entering several figures into an Excel file while a great noise of traffic and music comes in from outside. I ask Sarah why she decided to hang that … nursery rhyme on the wall. She tells me the reason is very simple: "It's about what we do every day. About everybody's work. And I love being operational, going into the field, going into companies, and interviewing workers. But my job, which I love, also involves a lot of time in here in July. … And so, if I happen to be bored or unmotivated, I read it, and I smile." (Field note, July 2017)

For the same reason, many inspectors hung their children's drawings on the wall. The regulations also prohibit information sharing: One cannot discuss cases with colleagues who are not working on the same case. Nevertheless, consulting with a colleague often also became a way of not only resolving specific cases by seeking advice but also a way of sharing the burden that comes with handling sensitive situations (Raaphorst & Loyens, 2020).

> "Confrontation for me is indispensable," Pino tells me. "Even if not really allowed. So, you ask things, but you tell half-truths. You don't name names, but you make your point. You squint your eyes, make strange nods, and close the office door." (Field note, September 2017)

> Gregorio walk[s] into Fausto's office and ask[s], "Listen, for that thing, about that worker, about that company, what about it? What do you think I should do? Do I get the worker to come first?" … When Gregorio leaves, I ask Fausto what he thinks of this coded way of asking for advice. Fausto, a new manager, laughs, saying that Gregorio and … "older inspectors" like him do this. However, Fausto feels freer to talk and share information with colleagues. "Because only in this way do we manage to unify, to understand what is … right. It is the most useful way to solve things. And … if you think

about it, workers complain more if we don't solve their problems than if we talk about them." (Field note, July 2017)

The sharing of information about cases was observed often within the offices. This created a "community of practice" (Wenger & Snyder, 2000) that acted on both a parallel and complementary plane to the formal one, helping to shape not only the choice of individual cases but also the procedures and practices of the office in general. This horizontal distribution of the weight of certain decisions, especially those that are highly discretionary, served as a way for inspectors to collectively read a new rule or a particular practice, thus sharing a uniform conception of interventions and reducing the risk of making formal errors (Paraciani & Saruis, 2019).

Behind closed doors, these offices also became containers of discontent for colleagues or managers. Most of these conversations originated from disagreements with how others handled certain disputes or final decisions. Recurring statements included "I wouldn't have done it that way" and "If I had done it myself" (field notes).

To observe different rooms of discretion led to the following preliminary considerations:

1. Pressures in policy directions related to workplace irregularity controls have increased the standardisation of procedures;
2. Pressures are aimed at accountability, resulting in inspectors being pushed to solve the highest number of cases with minimal waste of resources;[2]
3. Public pressures are classified as priorities for action or perceptions of the severity of cases, leading to some areas being neglected and some types of workers being given less attention;
4. Certain characteristics of street-level bureaucrats, such as their gender, years of experience, and type of studies conducted, create differences in the way work irregularities are handled.

In order to deepen these preliminary considerations and to understand how important these were to the professional role played by labour inspectors or the outcome of specific characteristics with which this professional

[2] Special reference is made here to the consequences of the transposition of the market model to the public sector, whereby public administrations are increasingly adopting tools and logic particular to private enterprises in line with the New Public Management paradigm.

role is exercised within organisational contexts, a comparison was conducted within two different institutional settings that constitute the organisational field in which labour inspectors operate. The technique used was that of vignettes, which is explained in the next section.

References

Brodkin, E. Z. (2008). Accountability in street-level organizations. *Journal of Public Administration, 31*(3), 317–336.

Bryman, A. (2016). *Social research methods.* Oxford University Press.

Cardano, M. (2011). *La ricerca qualitativa.* Il mulino.

Cottino, A. (2005). *Disonesto ma non criminale: la giustizia ei privilegi dei potenti.* Carocci.

Dubois, V. (2010). *The bureaucrat and the poor: Encounters in French welfare offices.* Routledge.

FRA. (2015). *Severe labour exploitation: Workers moving within or into the European Union. States' obligations and victims' rights*, Vienna.

Hasenfeld, Y., Rafferty, J. A., & Zald, M. N. (1987). The welfare state, citizenship, and bureaucratic encounters. *Annual Review of Sociology, 13*(1), 387–415.

Hupe, P. (2013). Dimensions of discretion: Specifying the object of street-level bureaucracy research. *Der Moderne Staat, 6*, 425–440.

Leonardi, D., Paraciani, R., & Raspanti, D. (2021). A strategy is necessary. The policy–client conflict within different relational asymmetries: A comparison at the street-level. *International Journal of Sociology and Social Policy, 41*(13/14), 81–95.

Marradi, A. (2007). *Metodologia delle scienze sociali.* Il mulino.

Maxwell, J. A. (2013). *Qualitative research design: An interactive approach.* Sage.

Merton, R. K. (1940). Fact and factitiousness in ethnic opinionnaires. *American Sociological Review, 5*(1), 13–28.

Mik-Meyer, N., & Silverman, D. (2019). Agency and clientship in public encounters: Co-constructing 'neediness' and 'worthiness' in shelter placement meetings. *The British Journal of Sociology, 70*(5), 1640–1660.

Paraciani, R., & Saruis, T. (2019). When the law is not enough. Caseworkers' ideas of justice in practices. *Sociologia del Lavoro, 152*, 163–182.

Raaphorst, N., & Loyens, K. (2020). From poker games to kitchen tables: How social dynamics affect frontline decision making. *Administration & Society, 52*(1), 31–56.

Semi, G. (2010). *L'osservazione partecipante. Una guida pratica*, Il mulino.

Silverman, D., & Marvasti, A. (2008). *Doing qualitative research: A comprehensive guide.* Sage.

Tummers, L. L., Bekkers, V., Vink, E., & Musheno, M. (2015). Coping during public service delivery: A conceptualization and systematic review of the literature. *Journal of Public Administration Research and Theory, 25*(4), 1099–1126.
Weber, M. (1997). *Storia economica: linee di una storia universale dell'economia e della società* (Vol. 5). Donzelli Editore.
Wenger, E. C., & Snyder, W. M. (2000). Communities of practice: The organizational frontier. *Harvard Business Review, 78*(1), 139–146.
Zacka, B. (2017). *When the state meets the street: Public service and moral agency.* Harvard University Press.
Zamperini, A. (1998). *Psicologia sociale della reponsabilità: giustizia, politica, etica e altri scenari.* UTET libreria.

CHAPTER 5

Isomorphic Pressures and Discretion: The Use of Vignettes in Interpretative Research

Abstract This chapter examines how labour inspectors' discretion is used within the coercive, mimetic, and normative institutional pressures present within the organisational field of workplace controls. Using the vignette technique, three productive sectors are compared: the domestic work sector, the logistics sector, and the restaurant sector. All of these sectors are productive and had the most irregularities, and all three sectors were characterised by precarious, low-paid, and socially penalising jobs as well as the presence of low-skilled and foreign workers. Logistics, restaurant, and domestic work differ in the role they play within the public sector. On the one hand, the logistics sector has been at the centre of the public agenda in recent years in part because of workers' growing ability to organise, resulting in it becoming an emergency sector. On the other hand, the domestic sector is not an "agenda-setting" one, and the severe isolation of female workers often makes the presence of a collective identity difficult. There are three main types of isomorphic pressures in the organisational field of workplace controls that clearly affect the ways in which inspectors interpret their discretionary space.

Keywords Vignette study • Work irregularities • Logistics sector • Domestic sector • Restaurant sector • Institutional pressures

R. Paraciani, *Labour Inspectors in Italy*,
https://doi.org/10.1007/978-3-031-37997-0_5

5.1 Vignettes in the Study of Labour Inspectors' Discretion

Vignettes have been used as an investigative tool in several disciplines, including sociology, marketing, and psychology (Saruis, 2015). They are constructed situations that encapsulate what the researcher has found through their field research. Three vignettes were constructed for this study using the ethnographic observations and preliminary considerations. The risk of using this interview technique is that respondents are led to describe a desirable reality (Finch, 1987). Therefore, it is necessary to create situations that are as realistic as possible, and the scenarios must offer interviewees the opportunity to recognise themselves in the resolution of cases they encounter during their work (Barberis, 2010). Vignettes are a very flexible research tool (Barter & Renold, 2000) as they can be easily adapted to different contexts. Discussing the cases proposed by the researcher allows for an open dialogue about the ways in which professionals conduct themselves, thereby overcoming the barrier of confidentiality. Respondents are asked to provide an interpretation of the hypothetical cases and simulate a decision-making process (Barberis, 2010). Scenarios can be in the form of pictures, text, or other stimuli so as to stimulate reactions, allowing researchers to gather precise information on reasoning, judgments, attitudes, and perceptions. After the stimulus is administered, the respondent is asked to imagine and reason about their experience by stating how the scenario's central character behaves.

Vignettes are used in both quantitative and qualitative research, with respondents having to choose their response from a multiple-choice list of possible answers in quantitative, experimental research (Bloor & Wood, 2006). In both qualitative and quantitative research, to stimulate realistic responses, the cases described in the scenario must be relevant and consistent with the respondents' experiential background; the more realistic the vignettes, the more realistic the responses (Finch, 1987; Wilks, 2004). Usually, researchers develop several vignettes to study different and changing situations (Barter & Renold, 2000; Barberis, 2010; Møller, 2016) to understand whether the introduction of new stimuli and new variables changes participants' responses and in what ways (Finch, 1987).

Vignettes can be a very useful tool in street-level bureaucracy research. First, because they are unobtrusive, they facilitate access to information, limiting the physical intrusion of the researcher into the context and protecting the respondents' confidentiality (Leonardi, 2021). Given the difficulty of operationalising certain concepts, using vignettes allowed the researcher to gain an understanding of small bureaucrats' perspectives by focusing on specific dilemmas (Saruis, 2015). Therefore, in this case, vignettes were a useful tool for testing hypotheses, verifying preliminary results, and extending the analysis to multiple levels, from the micro level to the macro level via the meso level (Møller, 2016).

In this research, the data collected during the nine months of participant observation were sorted, synthesised, labelled, and transformed into valuable information, which created additional questions. The research aimed to understand why similar labour irregularities are handled differently by labour inspectors in terms of the pressures from the organisational field in which they operate. Ethnographic research was conducted, from which preliminary considerations emerged that were subsequently tested and explored through semi-structured interviews. Three plausible scenarios were then constructed relative to labour inspectors' daily experiences, which were determined by asking them about their interventions when reporting labour irregularities that existed on the border between severe and non-severe forms of exploitation according to the exploitation pyramid (Fig. 3.1).

The work irregularities detailed in the calls for action and subsequently reproduced in the vignettes were similar in the three scenarios and concerned the following aspects: (a) lack of pay, (b) work isolation, (c) an employer's attempt at constant control both during work and during breaks, (d) working hours being longer than those stipulated by national collective bargaining agreements, and (e) lack of rest. The first call for action came from Mario, an Italian dishwasher, the second involved Alina, a domestic worker from Romania, and the third case included Paci, a tractor-trailer driver of Albanian origin. After the presentation of the scenarios, the conversation was guided by semi-structured questions without limiting interviewees from going "off track," from which useful additional information emerged. During the interviews, the labour inspectors were asked to explain how they handled requests for action (starting from the complaints desk and moving to reconstructing the decision-making chain to highlight how workers are perceived), how rules and procedures are interpreted (e.g., in terms of fairness and justice), and how the main dilemmas of their daily work are resolved. The inspectors were also asked to compare the most serious calls for action in terms of the similarities and differences in the treatment and management of this scenario.

The vignettes proved to be a useful tool because the field notes collected were very rich and detailed, which created difficulties in choosing the aspects that were to be the focus of the vignettes. The vignettes made it possible to focus on particular cases that had been observed in the first phase of the research, from which the preliminary findings were tested and further investigated. Beginning the interview with the administration of similar cases positively influenced the atmosphere of the discussion by encouraging spontaneous references to real cases.

The labour irregularities that inspectors are confronted with on a daily basis border non-severe forms of labour exploitation that are not prosecutable under criminal law and severe ones. These types of irregularities, as included in Article 603bis of the Italian Criminal Code, are as follows: (a) repeated payment of wages that are blatantly different from what is stipulated in national collective agreements; (b) repeated violations related to working hours, expectations, and vacations; (c) lack of compliance with safety and hygiene regulations in the workplace; and (d) degrading working conditions, surveillance methods, and housing situations.

The analysis focuses on and compares three different sectors: domestic work, logistics, and restaurant. Table 5.1 shows the labour irregularities observed, divided into sector and the rooms of discretion used (see Chap. 4).

Irregularities were observed in all three of these productive sectors: 42 in the domestic work sector; 27 in the logistics sector; and 35 in the restaurant sector. All three sectors have characteristics of what Piore (1979) calls the secondary sector: precarious, low-paid, and socially penalising jobs that are mainly characterised by the presence of low-skilled and foreign labour. There are three main types of isomorphic pressures acting in the organisational field of workplace controls, and they clearly affect the ways in which inspectors interpret their discretionary space: coercive, normative, and mimetic.

Table 5.1 The observed labour irregularities by sector and room of discretion

	Complaints desk	*Dispute-settlement procedure room*	*Labour inspectors' offices*	*Total*
Domestic work	12	28	2	42
Logistics	14	4	9	27
Restaurant	17	11	7	35

5.2 Coercive Isomorphism and Labour Inspectors' Discretion

As noted above, isomorphic pressures within the organisational field of workplace controls have led to the increased standardisation and simplification of the practices and procedures followed by labour inspectors. Among the main innovations introduced at the organisational level, resolving disputes through dispute-settlement procedures is an administrative mode of conflict resolution provided for by Legal Decree 124/2004 that had only recently (since 2014) became practice within the observed headquarters. The decision to find solutions here corresponds to coercive isomorphic pressures as it is a practice that speeds up the process, takes less time than the traditional inspection process, and offers workers the opportunity to obtain money in a shorter time. The Inspectorate mandates that all workers be offered the conciliatory solution as early as the complaint stage. However, in the face of this isomorphic pressure, inspectors used their discretionary spaces differently. The first differentiation emerged in relation to the production sector in which the labour irregularity occurred and labour inspectors' tendency to propose and advise for or against the conciliatory solution at the complaint stage.

As shown in Table 5.2, 12 labour irregularities involving domestic workers were observed, there were 14 requests for action within the logistics sector, and 17 complaints of workers experiencing one or more irregularities within the restaurant sector were filed at the complaints desk. In line with institutional pressures, the conciliatory solution was proposed in almost all cases, particularly in all cases involving domestic workers for whom the conciliatory solution was proposed at the complaint stage, recommended, and accepted by the workers, who considered it "the only

Table 5.2 The proposal of the dispute-settlement procedure by production sector

	Number of irregularities observed at the complaints desk	*Proposed*	*Recommended*	*Not recommended*	*Accepted by the worker*
Domestic work	12	12	12	0	12
Logistics	14	7	5	9	3
Restaurant	17	15	15	2	11

glimmer of hope when the home is the workplace" (field note) as it allowed them to obtain compensation in the shortest possible time. The prevalence of this procedure was also demonstrated by the data: The number of reported cases of wrongdoing for which an investigation and inspection procedure was initiated was 47 in 2015, but it plummeted to 1 in 2016, the year in which conciliation was introduced.[1] Since then, the conciliatory solution has become commonplace in the domestic work sector, regardless of the type of irregularity, thus reducing the likelihood of legal disputes related to the interpretation of the home as a place of work and an inviolable space that it is constitutionally protected (Art. 14, Italian Constitution). Even though Article 2113 of the Civil Code states that the violation of workers' rights should not be remedied by a simple economic settlement (as is the case with conciliation), this solution has become a standardised and legitimised procedure.

> Augustine tells me that they can't help everyone and that, when the work is domestic, there is always a risk that the investigation will end up being a "dead end." This is because "It is difficult to enter people's homes" and not everyone allows you to enter. Thus, the conciliatory solution is easier and allows for cases to be closed more quickly. (Field note, July 2017)

The same treatment is not given to labour irregularities within the logistics sector. Only seven out of 14 workers who filed a complaint were offered the conciliation route, and in two of the seven cases in which it was offered, the conciliatory solution was explained but discouraged. In this case, the inspectors act in line with coercive pressure, and their discretion was more far reaching.

> The worker, who is of Albanian origin, is a porter and is reporting some irregularities related to non-payment of the last few months' wages. He is employed within a cooperative, but the situation is very similar to the previous case involving a domestic worker. David explains to him … the possibility of conciliation but specifies that it does not suit the worker because he is entitled to more money than he could get in conciliation and because the cooperative would have no sanctions should it accept the conciliatory solution.

[1] Data on each INL territorial office can be found at the following link: www.ispettorato.gov.it/it-it/studiestatistiche.

> I ask David why, despite the similarity between the two cases, he proposed dispute-settlement procedure as the only possible solution in the former, while advising against it in the latter case. He tells me that "Now, logistics is in the eye of the storm" and is therefore a priority of the territorial headquarters. This means that inspectors have to reach a certain number of inspected companies in the logistics sector each year, so they have to "be present" and "do as many inspections as possible." (Field note, April 2017)

Of the 17 labour irregularities reported by workers within the restaurant industry, 15 were referred to conciliation, of which this practice was explained to two of them but was discouraged because they were two large companies and not family businesses, as with the other cases. When analysing the responses given to the interviews conducted using the vignette method, the results were similar: All respondents proposed a dispute-settlement procedure as the solution to the hypothetical case of Alina, regardless of the type of irregularity. The introduction of this practice also affected the way domestic work cases are perceived by inspectors as all of them referred to Alina's as the least serious case.

> I would choose to settle Alina's case first, so that she can get her dues according to the little evidence she has using the one-on-one conciliation procedure ... because having an inspector spend time to go and check on a domestic work is energy that should not be wasted on a case that can be settled in conciliation. (Interview 9)

> If I could, I would choose Alina's case without a second thought. Using the dispute-settlement procedure means ... it's as good as settled. We have a chance to find a quick solution and close the case, so we can spend time on other things. (Interview 3)

> If I found Paci in front of me (and we see Pacis every day, by the way), I would tell him that he can [use conciliation and] explain ... what it is, but then I would tell him why, in my opinion, he should not agree to dispute settlement procedure: He should not do it because he is an exploited worker in an exploitative industry. Because the more Paci[s] we help and the more companies where Paci[s] work we inspect, the greater the scope of our results. If I were to find Alina (and I see Alinas on a daily basis as well), then I would propose conciliation to her as the only possible solution. Take the money and be thankful! (Interview 11)

In addition to the different considerations given to workers from the logistics and domestic work sectors in relation to labour irregularities, the problem of resources available to street-level bureaucrats should be considered. Deploying resources to inspect a warehouse or a cooperative within which many workers work would have a greater impact on the community than deploying the same resources in the domestic context, where inspection access is more strenuous and is limited to verifying the situation of single workers who are usually employed by one family each.

5.3 Mimetic Isomorphism and Labour Inspectors' Discretion

Mimetic pressures reduce uncertainties regarding the inspection outcomes by encouraging the adoption of standardised strategies (Paraciani & Rizza, 2021). As a result, there is a general tendency to use the conciliation procedure, which, in most situations, is the most expeditious solution. In the cases observed, this tendency was most evident in domestic work situations. There are several scholarly contributions that highlight how stereotypes have become entrenched in domestic work in Italy as these female workers, who are typically from Eastern Europe, are seen as "crafty" or "calculating" (field note; Catanzaro & Colombo, 2009; Fullin & Vercelloni, 2009). This limits the quality of the interactions between inspectors and domestic workers due to the reduced amount of time spent interacting with workers from the domestic work sector compared to other sectors and the limited options offered to female workers. Some inspectors were less committed to dealing with these cases, leading to them choosing the quickest and least demanding solution.

> During the [one-on-one] conciliation, Inspector Augustine is speaking in very technical language. The domestic worker, of Romanian origin, has become nervous and loudly accuses Augustine of not putting her in a position to be able to understand. "I don't understand, she talks [using advanced language] and doesn't leave me time to explain why I am here!" Augustine replies … "I speak this way because the law speaks this way, and if you do not understand the law, we cannot find a solution." (Field note, March 2017)

> In conciliation, the domestic worker, of Ukrainian origin, is accusing her employer of treating her like a slave. She is very agitated and, as she makes these accusations, she shows us [a photo on] her cell phone … of a single mattress lying on the floor that has been her bed for the past few months. Inspector Marika does not look at the photo because "this is not the place

to gather evidence," she says. She then suggests that [the domestic worker] "be okay with" the conciliatory solution. (Field note, April 2017)

During a coffee break, Gregorio and Serena are commenting on the increase in the number of domestic workers who come to the counter to report their irregular work status. Gregorio, in jest, says that … "word has gotten out" and that, with one-on-one conciliation, they are able to "get a few things" and that this is why they come here, "even exaggerating their situation." (Field note, May 2017)

In the observed labour irregularities in the restaurant sector, uncertainty was mainly manifested in relation to the consequences for the employer. In fact, in many of the cases (17 out of 35 total cases), labour inspectors expressed concerns about an inspection's consequences and penalising business owners. Thus, the conciliatory solution that economically addressed the irregularities (often those related to wages and contributions) without sanctioning the employer was preferred.

Simona tells me that the reason she often suggests conciliation to workers employed in the restaurant industry is that they … often work for small, family-owned businesses, for which the possibility of not incurring a penalty, [which is] a possibility that becomes a certainty if the parties reach an agreement, offers workers a better chance of being able to get "something," meaning monetary compensation, and … closing the case "without bringing small family businesses to their knees." (Field note, May 2017)

In part, this protection of the employer was also recorded in some cases in the domestic work sector (12 out of 42 cases). In contrast, this situation did not occur in the logistics sector.

The vignettes interviews demonstrate that the one-on-one conciliation procedure is the preferred choice for domestic workers and it is also the way in which the biggest differences emerged between the domestic work and logistics sectors. In the latter, when labour irregularities were reported in the Paci vignette, only two respondents proposed the conciliatory solution. This was the opposite of what was proposed by many inspectors (8/15) for Alina's case, even though the inspectors acknowledged that she was experiencing exploitation. Moreover, there was an additional difference in the way that the inspectors treated the domestic work case compared to the logistics case: Some expressed that Alina's request for intervention might be a way to gain benefits through conciliatory practices. This relates to the aforementioned existence of culturally entrenched beliefs and stereotypes about domestic workers that affect inspectors' personal assessments (Fullin & Vercelloni, 2009). In this case, mimetic pressures can, in a sense, be considered a protection in favour of the female worker.

> If the working hours are like this, Alina is being exploited, although I think she might be confusing it with providing companionship to the elderly person to be cared in her work. I mean, these things are hard to verify. It is better to conciliate. (Interview 4)

> If this claim were true, Alina would be exploited. But I would conciliate. However … the first thing I would do if conciliation did not exist in such a case is verify that Alina is not lying. (Interview 12)

Similar answers were not given by the inspectors when they were interviewed about similar irregularities in the logistics and restaurant sectors.

5.4 Normative Isomorphism and Labour Inspectors' Discretion

In addition to coercive and mimetic isomorphic pressures, the organisational field of workplace controls is also characterised by the presence of normative pressures. Isomorphism is normative when professionalisation is evolved to establish conditions and methods of work that are considered better than previous conditions, thereby legitimising them. In these cases, the change in practices is not generated by uncertainty but by the belief in the (presumed) superiority of specific practices (Bonazzi, 2002). In the present case, the regulatory pressures arose from the harmonisation of practices as a result of the direction taken by labour inspectors' professionalisation. Nevertheless, labour inspectors adopt different approaches in relation to their experiences of the current changes in the profession. Indeed, the ethnographic survey revealed a difference between senior and junior labour inspectors: Although the pressures acting on the organisational field of workplace controls encourage the adoption of standardised practices and the use of administrative as well as less resource- and energy-intensive solutions, senior labour inspectors did not follow this trend.

> "I've been doing this job for 19 years," Rossana tells me, "and 19 years is a really long time. Frankly, I'm not very comfortable with people who have no

> experience in the field telling me how I should do my job solely because they've read ... books [on] how it should be done." (Field note, June 2017, Rossana, senior labour inspector)

> Savio is drinking his coffee, shaking his head contritely. He tells me that, lately, after 20 years of service, he sometimes feels that he does not understand the meaning of his own work. "From 1996 to 2004, we were doing eight inspections every day. Everything was simple: There is a request for action, I start the investigation to look for evidence, interview people, and [mete out] justice. The procedures were simple. Now, however, we have to waste I can't imagine how much time on paperwork and bureaucratic affairs. We have become administrators." (Field note, September 2017, Savio, senior labour inspector)

Junior labour inspectors, unlike senior inspectors, must hold a university degree in political science, economics, or law, and they become inspectors after winning an open public competition. Upon entering the service, part of the professional training is informal, including shadowing senior inspectors, but another requirement is completing courses. These inspectors are urged to consider the efficiency of their actions as the main goal of their work, understood as solving the greatest number of cases in the shortest possible time through standardised practices and administrative solutions.

> At the complaints desk, Augustine tells me that he is happy when domestic work cases come in because "they are always easy. You don't have to think too hard, and you don't have a choice: Dispute settlement procedure is always the right solution." (Field note, March 2017, Augustine, junior labour inspector)

> Fausto is very pleased that accountability practices have been introduced in the observed territorial location that make activity measurable. He goes on to tell me that senior labour inspectors feel limited by the fact that there are standards to be achieved, whereas, in his opinion, numbers are necessary to communicate what they do. Not only inter-regionally and nationally but also to citizens who have the opportunity to ... see how much they work. (Field note, September 2017, Fausto, junior labour inspector)

Another indicator of effectiveness introduced by normative isomorphic pressures is the social impact of a practice, which leads to the consideration of the reach that a given action has for society as a whole. This element is also considered by the new generation of labour inspectors, which translates into the different ways of perceiving the seriousness of situations between senior and junior inspectors. For example, the latter perceive more severe cases within productive sectors as part of territorial priorities and believe that they result in a kind of "good example." A restaurant or logistics enterprise is considered more important than domestic work, so an inspection would affect more people. This tendency has also manifested itself among senior inspectors, but they also tend to place more emphasis on the uniqueness of each case. This is also the reason why cases that require discretion being used "out of the law" (i.e., violating formal regulations) have been recorded only among senior labour inspectors.

> I am at the complaints desk with Inspector Marika. A worker of Moldavian origin, a tractor-trailer driver, came to complain that he had not received his latest wages and [was being] blackmailed … by his employer. The cooperative he works for used to send him information regarding the warehouses in which [he had] to load and unload goods on a daily basis via text message. Not only did he not receive his last five paycheques, but he was [also] monitored in relation to the pace of work and was required to take as few breaks as possible.
>
> Marika explains to me that this is a very sensitive case because, if they go to check the tachograph of the tractor-trailer and it turns out … that the mandatory breaks have not been observed … the worker would also suffer a hefty penalty. [Marika] takes notes, verifies information on her computer twice, and thinks about it for a moment. She turns to the worker [and says], "Let's do this: You never came. I'll write down everything: the name of the cooperative and the information you gave me, but we'll make it an anonymous report because, otherwise, you're also at great risk." She [then] explains the regulations and situation to him in detail, takes the necessary information, and lets him go. I ask her why she made this decision [and flouted] a regulation. She tells me that there are situations where you have to understand people, and this is one of them. Turning a blind eye, in this case, means taking the side of the worker who would otherwise be "cuckolded." (Field note, September 2017, Marika, senior labour inspector)

> During the one-on-one conciliation, the Ukrainian-born domestic worker is not speaking and there is … silence in the room. She seems intimidated by the presence of her employer, who does not even look at her face. Rosanna seems unnerved that this lack of communication is getting the conciliation nowhere. She then decides to make the employer leave the room, despite

the fact that procedure does not allow it. Once out, the worker breaks the silence by bursting into tears. She complains that not only that she has not been paid, but ... that she has been sexually abused, showing bruises on her body. Rosanna decides to proceed on a dual track: to pursue conciliation to get the worker "at least some economic independence quickly" and to contact law enforcement herself, pursuing criminal proceedings in parallel. She later points out to me that, if she had not broken that rule, the conciliation would have been "a washout." (Field note, March 2017, Rosanna, senior labour inspector)

Consistent with the findings of the observations, the vignettes also show that it is predominantly senior inspectors who act in ways that are not perfectly in line with what is expected.

A: "When ... a worker like Paci ... files a complaint there are two things to do: Firstly, you propose the dispute-settlement procedure, and secondly ... you disempower the worker. I want to see the logistics for myself."

Q: "What about when Alina is the whistle-blower?"

A: "When reporting, I would do the same with Alina, but in a more veiled way. I ... have been doing this work for many years, and I prefer to go and see, even in cases where you have to ask permission." (Interview 12, A senior labour inspector)

Only the senior inspectors were willing to "turn a blind eye" (interview 15) so as not to incentivise the use of the administrative solution, and they would do so in both Alina's and Paci's cases. Among the nine junior inspectors who participated in the interview, however, only three would be willing to turn a blind eye, and only in Paci's case.

I would recommend the dispute settlement procedure in both cases. In Alina's case, I would present it as the only possible solution, and in Paci's case, on the other hand, I would point out to him that an inspection of the company could reveal many more situations ... and this could help many workers who have not had ... the courage to complain like him. (Interview 3, A junior labour inspector)

In Paci's case, I would advise against conciliating for one simple reason: There are many more Pacis and far fewer Alinas in the same workplace. (Interview 1, A junior labour inspector)

References

Barberis, E. (2010). Rapporti territoriali e coordinamento. Una contestualizzazione della governance sociale in Italia. *La rivista delle politiche sociali, 1*, 79–101.

Barter, C., & Renold, E. (2000). 'I wanna tell you a story': Exploring the application of vignettes in qualitative research with children and young people. *International Journal of Social Research Methodology, 3*(4), 307–323.

Bloor, M., & Wood, F. (2006). *Keywords in qualitative methods: A vocabulary of research concepts*. Sage.

Bonazzi, G. (2002). *Come studiare le organizzazioni*. Il Mulino.

Catanzaro, R., & Colombo, A. (2009). *Badanti & Co. Il lavoro domestico straniero in Italia*. Il Mulino.

Finch, J. (1987). The vignette technique in survey research. *Sociology, 21*(1), 105–114.

Fullin, G., & Vercelloni, V. (2009). Dentro la trappola. Percezioni e immagini del lavoro domestico e di cura nei percorsi delle donne immigrate. *Polis, 23*(3), 427–462.

Leonardi, D. (2021). How to use the vignette technique to uncover judgments, values, relationships with norms. Methodological reflections from a research project on professional discretion. *Sociologia Italiana–AIS Journal of Sociology, 18*, 53–68.

Møller, M. Ø. (2016). 'She isn't someone I associate with pension'. A vignette study of professional reasoning. *Professions & Professionalism, 6*(1), 1–20.

Paraciani, R., & Rizza, R. (2021). When the workplace is the home: Labour inspectors' discretionary power in the field of domestic work–An institutional analysis. *Journal of Public Policy, 41*(1), 1–16.

Piore, M. J. (1979). *Birds of passage: Migrant labor in industrial societies*. Cambridge University Press.

Saruis, T. (2015). *Gli operatori sociali nel nuovo welfare: tra discrezionalità e responsabilità*. Carocci editore.

Wilks, T. (2004). The use of vignettes in qualitative research into social work values. *Qualitative Social Work, 3*(1), 78–87.

CHAPTER 6

Conclusion

Abstract This chapter aims to move beyond the current street-level research, which often separates and contrasts micro and macro analysis. Furthermore, the street-level theory is often used in Northern European or Anglo-Saxon contexts, but it has been proven to be an excellent tool for studying different contexts, such as Mediterranean Europe, which are contexts characterised by fragmented welfare systems and low trust in institutions. One of the most important findings concerns the ways in which different paths of professionalisation affect the ways in which inspectors make decisions that are reflected in differentiated operational practices. Moreover, to return the street-level approach to its comparative essence, additional possibilities for areas of in-depth study are provided. This research compares the management of similar work irregularities within different productive sectors, but the comparison can go further by involving different contexts. In this sense, a vignette can be a useful methodological tool. The same can be said of the organisational field, which can prove useful for counteracting the territorial differences that often make comparisons in street-level research difficult.

Keywords Street-level bureaucracy • Labour inspectors • Discretion • Neo-institutionalism • Isomorphic pressures

R. Paraciani, *Labour Inspectors in Italy*,
https://doi.org/10.1007/978-3-031-37997-0_6

The general purpose of this work has been to contribute to the knowledge on the complex relationship between citizens' needs and the services they obtain from public administration in its different articulations and areas of intervention. When a policeman asks for a document, when having to undergo an interview to access a certain training course, and when applying for unemployment benefits, bureaucracy stops being abstract and becomes something concrete. Or, rather, someone becomes concrete: a person who, while occupying intermediate hierarchical levels, has influence and acts as a decision-maker by making choices that will lead to tangible results for citizens. In particular, this relationship was investigated by placing a particular and understudied category of street-level bureaucrats at the centre of the research: labour inspectors. The purpose was to investigate their operational practices and the ways in which they resolve similar labour irregularities according to different places and productive sectors.

Addressing Rice's (2019) statement, two theoretical approaches that were developed on parallel tracks were integrated: street-level bureaucracy and neo-institutionalism. This was in order to understand how the labour inspectors employ discretion within the organisational field of workplace controls.

The research questions that guided this study are as follows: (a) What institutional pressures exist in the organisational field of workplace controls, and what are their consequences? (b) How does labour inspectors' discretion manifest in their interventions, and what impact does it have in terms of determining the severity of the cases handled? (c) Why are similar labour irregularities treated differently?

After presenting the literature in the second chapter and detailing the Italian case study in the third, Chaps. 4 and 5 focused on the results of this three-year-long study. First, through nine months of participant observation in a local office of the Italian National Labour Inspectorate, I accessed the places where discretion is exercised and highlighted the different modes of action and the different decisions made in the face of different isomorphic pressures. Although the literature on street-level bureaucracy attaches great importance to the bureaucratic meeting between the street-level bureaucrat and the worker, which represents the moment that the state confronts citizens' concrete problems, thereby giving meaning to the law (Tummers et al., 2015; Raspanti, 2019), little attention has been paid to the ergonomics of the spaces in which this encounter takes place (Zacka, 2017). The spatial configuration of the office observed was used to delineate these street-level bureaucrats' work and choices and to highlight the different moments of the bureaucratic encounter, thereby demonstrating the different methods of conflict management and the various decision-making styles. In fact, although special organisation is of great importance for the methods and outcomes of interventions, it is often a dimension neglected both in the planning of services and in research. The spatial configuration of the venue observed was used, on the one hand, as a pretext to narrate the work and choices of these street-level bureaucrats, but also to highlight the different moments of the bureaucratic encounter, shedding light on the different conflict management and decision-making styles. The organisation of space contributes to translating political choices and choices of practices into practice.

Starting with the description of these locations, the modalities of the bureaucratic encounters between the users and inspectors were analysed for each of the procedure's stages. This entailed an examination of the inspectors' tasks, the various characteristics of the interactions and discourse, the possible choices, and the ways in which disputes were handled. Similar work irregularities were handled in different ways both at the complaint desk and at the dispute-settlement procedure stage. In the back-office phase, the operational differences were related to the ways in which information was shared between inspectors, with particular emphasis on the differences in the handling of similar work irregularities depending on the production sector. The finding that deserves further research is the idea that the spatial organisation supports institutional dynamics and reflects on the quality of the interaction between the service and the citizen. Observing these dynamics can highlight how different levels of social interaction and decision-making recur in spatial configurations (Lascoumes & Le Galès, 2007). Thus, the organisation of space helps to translate political choices into practice.

I then attempted to explain the differences that emerged within the organisational field of workplace controls in which different institutional pressures are active. This book aims to connect the analytical tools provided by the strand of street-level bureaucracy research that exists within neo-institutionalist sociological theory (Powell & DiMaggio, 2012). This was achieved by asking the following questions: To what extent is street-level bureaucrats' discretion influenced by the institutional pressures of the organisational field of workplace controls? What are these pressures, and how is inspectors' discretion oriented on the basis of these pressures?

The ethnographic study, in fact, highlighted that similar work irregularities were handled using different methods. Particularly, a difference was noted in the management of similar work irregularities according to the productive sector. These differences were explored in the last chapter using vignette technique, which were interpreted according to the organisational field of workplace controls in which different institutional pressures are active. The aim was to connect the analytical tools provided by street-level bureaucracy studies with those belonging to neo-institutionalist sociological theory. For this reason, three comparable scenarios were created and presented to 15 labour inspectors. Each scenario represented the same work irregularity in different productive sectors and with different workers. These scenarios included complaints from three workers: Alina, Paci, and Mario. These complaints were similar but were based within three different production sectors: domestic work, logistics, and catering. These production sectors are the ones in which the most irregularities were observed, and they are characterised by precarious, low-paid, and socially penalising jobs that are mostly filled by low-skilled labour and foreigners. These sectors differ in the roles they play within the public discourse. On the one hand, the logistics sector has been at the centre of the public agenda in recent years (partly due to workers' capacity to organise) and has become an emergency sector. On the other hand, the domestic sector is not an agenda-setting sector, and the significant isolation of female workers in this sector often makes collective bargaining difficult (Sarti, 2010).

Reasoning in terms of the organisational field of workplace controls allowed for the analysis of the labour inspectors' discretion in relation to the broader institutional context and the isomorphic pressures that influence it, including coercive, mimetic, and normative pressures (Paraciani & Rizza, 2021).

Coercive isomorphic pressure was first highlighted, which translated into the tendency to adopt standardised strategies that are oriented to the quantitative goals of effectiveness and efficiency. Mimetic isomorphic pressure resulted in uncertainty, and normative isomorphic pressure was reflected in the different ways in which inspectors with different career paths, who were labelled as "senior" and "junior" inspectors herein, handled similar work irregularities. Despite this, the identified pressures did not eliminate the inspectors' discretionary spaces.

Faced with coercive pressures from above, inspectors' different uses of discretionary space emerged. An initial differentiation came to light in relation to the production sector in which the labour irregularity occurred and labour inspectors' tendency to propose and advise for or against the conciliatory solution at the complaint stage. In particular, while this solution was recommended in the restaurant sector and encouraged in domestic work, the same is not true for logistics, which was the sector in which inspectors were more inclined to initiate a traditional inspection. In addition to the different weights given to logistics and domestic work in terms of labour irregularities, the resources available to street-level bureaucrats must be considered. Allocating resources to inspections of warehouses or cooperatives that include many workers would have a greater impact on the community than allocating the same amount of resources to the domestic sector, where access is more difficult and limited to reviewing a single worker's situation, who is often employed by a single family. When the pressures are mimetic, the results of discretionary action are similar, but the reasons leading to that decision are different: The dispute-settlement procedure tends to be encouraged for domestic workers for economic reasons as reconciliation requires fewer resources from the inspectorate. However, when the isomorphism is mimetic, the quickest and least demanding solution is chosen due to the stereotypes and false beliefs that exist about domestic workers, which is seen as 'smart' (field note). This limits the quality of the interaction as less time is given to these cases than to others, resulting in fewer options being offered to domestic workers. There are also regulatory pressures in the organisational field of workplace controls, which result from the harmonisation of practices due to the direction taken by the professionalisation of labour inspectors. Nevertheless, labour inspectors adopt different approaches precisely because of their different experiences with the changes in the profession. Indeed, the ethnographic survey revealed a difference between the senior and junior labour inspectors. Even though organisational pressures encourage the adoption of standardised practices and the use of administrative solutions that are less resource- and energy-intensive, senior labour inspectors did not follow this trend: The senior inspectors interviewed were willing to "turn a blind eye" (interview 15) in terms of encouraging the use of administrative solutions for the three cases considered. However, among the nine junior inspectors interviewed, only three were willing to turn a blind eye and only for the logistics case study.

One of the most important findings that emerged concerns the ways in which different professionalisation paths affect how inspectors make decisions that are reflected in differentiated operational practices. Therefore, the transformations of professions and professionals in the face of increasing standardisation of practices needs to be studied by asking the following question: Is standardisation a guarantee of protection and uniformity of treatment in the face of regulations, or does it risk deteriorating the quality of the bureaucratic encounter?

Moreover, additional possibilities for in-depth study were identified for returning the street-level approach to its comparative essence. This study focused on the different ways in which similar cases that occurred within different productive sectors were handled. All of the sectors considered, however, belong to the secondary area of the labour market. Therefore, the occurrences in less peripheral areas of the labour market, where more nuanced elements of labour exploitation are present and sometimes more frequent need to be investigated by asking how inspectors respond and if intervention policies change. Moreover, comparative research could be conducted to expand on this study by analysing different territories to determine the differences that exist in different labour markets, the prevalence of undeclared work, and labour inspectors' typical interventions. In this sense, the organisational field of workplace controls could be used to reduce the weight of the differences and to allow for the comparison of strikingly different territories. This can be done by asking the following questions: Does widespread undeclared work make labour inspectors more tolerant or stricter? How does understaffing in relation to requests for intervention affect the way cases are resolved? Does the introduction of standardised procedures signal something important in our country's labour culture? Lastly, emotional labour should be considered (Hochschild, 2002; Demertzis, 2020) by placing labour inspectors' detachment and emotional involvement at the centre of investigation.

The originality of this study derives from the context of the research as public policies in Italy are still understudied from a street-level perspective, which is particularly interesting as this is a context in which welfare is fragmented and distrust of institutions and the public sector is high (Barberis et al., 2019; Lotta & Pires, 2023). Thus, it is proposed that the classic street-level theory can be advanced by using the neo-institutionalist approach to analyse decision-making processes, thereby favouring a multidimensional understanding of the phenomenon under investigation.

References

Barberis, E., Paraciani, R., & Saruis, T. (2019). Nota introduttiva al focus. *Social Policies, 6*(3), 389–406.

Demertzis, N. (2020). *The political sociology of emotions: Essays on trauma and ressentiment*. Routledge.

Hochschild, A. R. (2002). The sociology of emotion as a way of seeing. In G. Bendelow & J. S. Williams (Eds.), *Emotions in social life*. Routledge.

Lascoumes, P., & Le Galès, P. (2007). Understanding public policy through its instruments—From the nature of instruments to the sociology of public policy instrumentation. *Governance, 20*(1), 1–21.

Lotta, G., & Pires, R. (2023). Public Policy Implementation in a context of extreme inequality: Between universalist ambitions and practical selectivity. In E. Lisboa, R. Corrêa Gomes, & H. Falcao Martins (Eds.), *The Brazilian way of doing public administration: Brazil with An's'* (pp. 219–231). Emerald Publishing Limited.

Paraciani, R., & Rizza, R. (2021). When the workplace is the home: Labour inspectors' discretionary power in the field of domestic work–An institutional analysis. *Journal of Public Policy, 41*(1), 1–16.

Powell, W. W., & DiMaggio, P. J. (Eds.). (2012). *The new institutionalism in organizational analysis*. University of Chicago press.

Raspanti, D. (2019). Coping with a voluntary client. Frontline workers in public employment services dealing with employers' recruitment needs. *Social Policies, 6*(3), 427–446.

Rice, D. (2019). Adopting an institutional view in street-level bureaucracy research. In P. Hupe (Ed.), *Research handbook on street-level bureaucracy* (pp. 70–85). Edward Elgar Publishing.

Sarti, R. (2010). *Lavoro domestico e di cura: quali diritti?* Ediesse.

Tummers, L. L., Bekkers, V., Vink, E., & Musheno, M. (2015). Coping during public service delivery: A conceptualization and systematic review of the literature. *Journal of Public Administration Research and Theory, 25*(4), 1099–1126.

Zacka, B. (2017). *When the state meets the street: Public service and moral agency*. Harvard University Press.

Index[1]

[1] Note: Page numbers followed by 'n' refer to notes.

R. Paraciani, *Labour Inspectors in Italy*,
https://doi.org/10.1007/978-3-031-37997-0

FSC
www.fsc.org
MIX
Papier | Fördert
gute Waldnutzung
FSC® C083411

Kolibri 360 GmbH
Ferdinand-Jühlke-Straße 7
99095 Erfurt, Deutschland
produktsicherheit@kolibri360.de